S. Hrg. 113–474

STRENGTHENING U.S. ALLIANCES IN NORTHEAST ASIA

HEARING

BEFORE THE

SUBCOMMITTEE ON EAST ASIAN AND PACIFIC AFFAIRS

OF THE

COMMITTEE ON FOREIGN RELATIONS

UNITED STATES SENATE

ONE HUNDRED THIRTEENTH CONGRESS

SECOND SESSION

MARCH 4, 2014

Printed for the use of the Committee on Foreign Relations

Available via the World Wide Web: http://www.gpo.gov/fdsys/

U.S. GOVERNMENT PUBLISHING OFFICE

91–296 PDF   WASHINGTON : 2015

For sale by the Superintendent of Documents, U.S. Government Publishing Office
Internet: bookstore.gpo.gov   Phone: toll free (866) 512–1800; DC area (202) 512–1800
Fax: (202) 512–2104   Mail: Stop IDCC, Washington, DC 20402–0001

(II)

CONTENTS

STRENGTHENING U.S. ALLIANCES IN NORTHEAST ASIA

TUESDAY, MARCH 4, 2014

U.S. SENATE,
SUBCOMMITTEE ON EAST ASIAN AND PACIFIC AFFAIRS,
COMMITTEE ON FOREIGN RELATIONS,
Washington, DC.

The subcommittee met, pursuant to notice, at 2:57 p.m., in room SD–419, Dirksen Senate Office Building, Hon. Benjamin L. Cardin (chairman of the subcommittee) presiding.

Present: Senator Cardin.

OPENING STATEMENT OF HON. BENJAMIN L. CARDIN, U.S. SENATOR FROM MARYLAND

Senator CARDIN. Let me welcome you all to the Subcommittee on East Asian and Pacific Affairs' hearing, "Strengthening the U.S. Alliance in Northeast Asia."

I know that Senator Rubio, who had planned to be here today as the ranking Republican member, will not be able to be here due to the travel problems associated with the weather conditions. And, as some might be aware, because of that, scheduled votes today in the United States Senate have been postponed until tomorrow. So, it probably will mean we will not have as many of the members of our subcommittee present today as we would otherwise have, but I just want to assure, not only our witnesses, but also those who are following this hearing, the incredible importance of today's hearing of the subcommittee, not just for the Senate Foreign Relations Committee, but for the United States Senate.

This is our first hearing this year. Last year, we held a series of hearings dealing with the administration's "Rebalance to Asia" policy. We looked at it from a good governance standpoint, we evaluated its economic impact, and we also looked at the military security issues as well as environmental issues. We covered a lot of specific areas of interest that further demonstrated why the "Rebalance to Asia" is critically important for not only the administration, but also for Congress. So, we hope to assess how we are moving forward in regards to concrete actions and appropriate resources.

The U.S. alliance with Japan and the Republic of Korea serve as the centerpiece of U.S. engagement in Northeast Asia. How we work together and how the United States approaches and manages these relationships is vital to U.S. security interests and has important implications across the entire region.

In this hearing, we will evaluate the status and trajectory of U.S. relations with each of these key allies, and I hope to hear from our witnesses on areas where we should increase cooperation, both bilaterally and trilaterally.

Our alliance with Japan is the cornerstone of U.S. engagement in the region. Last October, Secretaries Kerry and Hagel held a historic meeting in Tokyo with their Japanese counterparts and released a joint statement reaffirming the alliance and defining steps to upgrade the capability of the partnership, including the announcement of a revision to the United States-Japan defense guidelines. In recent months, Japan established a National Security Council, adopted the National Security Strategy, and established the National Defense Program Guidelines. These actions are moving Japan toward a more active role in the international sphere and opening the door for a more robust alliance with the United States. There have been positive developments for the Futenma Replacement Facility since the Governor of Okinawa approved a landfill permit. But, clearly, more challenges remain. When I was in Japan, one of the centerpieces of our conversations was the future of United States presence in Okinawa and how that relates to our security arrangements. And there have been stalled efforts to move that forward. Some of that has created political issues, both in Japan and the United States. So, it was encouraging to see some positive developments.

In December, Congress passed the National Defense Authorization Act providing funding to make way for the eventual transfer of marines and their dependents from Japan to Guam and Hawaii. United States and Japan reached a milestone agreement in 2013, the U.S.-Japan Okinawa Consolidation Plan, which lays out details for consolidating and closing U.S. military bases in Okinawa and elsewhere in Japan, thereby reinforcing our efforts to modernize the alliance to meet emerging challenges in the region. And, of course, Japan announced last year that they would be joining the Trans-Pacific Partnership, TPP, negotiations, a step that was welcomed by the United States.

So, I hope at this hearing we can get more specifics on how we are moving forward on the security front and on the economic front with Japan.

In South Korea last year, we celebrated the 60th anniversary of the alliance. In May, President Park visited the United States, and it was an honor to have her address a joint session of Congress. And I had a chance to have a conversation with her and go over her vision on how to improve security arrangements in Northeast Asia. We had a good conversation, and she moved forward with the suggestion of developing an OSCE-type forum for Northeast Asia. South Korea is an important economic partner for the United States, particularly since the signing and implementation of the U.S.-Korea Free Trade Agreement in 2012. And it is promising to see South Korea's expression of interest in the Trans-Pacific Partnership.

In addition, our countries reached final agreement, earlier this month, on sharing the defense costs of U.S. troops stationed in South Korea. From cooperation on clean energy to supporting our mission in Afghanistan, this alliance has truly transformed into a global partnership.

Although we see these positive steps in our bilateral alliance, this region is home to some very serious challenges. North Korea continues down the path of belligerent and erratic behavior, including expanding its Yongbyon uranium enrichment facility, restarting the reactor, and displaying complete disregard for the welfare of its own people. China continues to make aggressive moves to stake its claim in the East China Sea, including the November announcement of a new Air Defense Identification Zone. Japan and South Korea remain deeply suspicious of one another, based on sensitive historical issues, and the Japanese Prime Minister's rhetoric on these issues is increasingly concerning to many. Additionally, fiscal constraints in the United States have raised questions among our allies about the potential impact on these important alliances. These are all issues I hope we will be able to address during this hearing.

These issues not only demand that we work closely with our allies and avoid surprises, but they also present opportunities to reinforce our bilateral and trilateral cooperation. We need to build on our successes, focus on shared goals, and continue to grow and expand our alliance in Northeast Asia to ensure each relationship reaches its full potential.

I hope President Obama will seek to reinforce these messages when he travels to the region again next month. I look forward to hearing from both our panels today on how we can be sure we are well postured from both a diplomatic and a strategic perspective in order to address these shared challenges.

And, with that, we will turn to our first panel, where we have our government witnesses. And we thank you both for being here.

Daniel Russel is no stranger to this committee, Assistant Secretary of State for the Bureau of East Asia and Pacific Affairs at the Department of State. Mr. Russel began his tour as an Assistant Secretary on July 13 of last year. He previously served at the White House as Special Assistant to the President and National Security Staff Senior Director for Asian Affairs.

We are also pleased to have with us today David F. Helvey, Deputy Assistant Secretary of Defense for East Asia in the Office of the Under Secretary of Defense for Policy. Previously, he served as the Acting Deputy Assistant Secretary of Defense and was a Principal Director for East Asia in the Office of the Assistant Secretary of Defense for Asia and Pacific Security Affairs, East Asia.

Welcome to you both. We will start with Mr. Russel.

STATEMENT OF HON. DANIEL RUSSEL, ASSISTANT SECRETARY FOR EAST ASIAN AND PACIFIC AFFAIRS, U.S. DEPARTMENT OF STATE, WASHINGTON, DC

Mr. RUSSEL. Chairman Cardin, thank you very much for the opportunity to appear today before you to discuss this important set of issues that you laid out in your introductory remarks.

I would like to request that my prepared statement be entered into the record.

Senator CARDIN. All the witnesses on both panels, their full statements will be made part of the record, so you may proceed as you wish.

Mr. RUSSEL. Thank you.

The Obama administration has made the Asia-Pacific a strategic priority, based on America's stake in a prosperous and stable region. And the Department of State is focused on dedicating diplomatic, public diplomacy, and assistance resources to the region commensurate with the priority and the comprehensive nature of our engagement.

From the outset, the governing principle of this administration's Asia rebalance policy has been to ensure close ties with our partners and allies. Our alliances with the Republic of Korea and with Japan contribute significantly to regional security, stability, and prosperity. These alliances are rooted in our shared strategic interests, our deep and growing economic ties, our shared values, and in extensive people-to-people connections.

I am pleased to report today, Mr. Chairman, that our alliances with both countries have never been stronger. We are working hard with our Japanese and South Korean partners to modernize these alliances and to address broader shared interests across the Asia-Pacific and around the globe. I want to thank you, Mr. Chairman, as well as members of the other subcommittee, for your leadership, your travel, and your public statements underscoring the importance of these alliances.

Let me speak briefly to each relationship.

The United States-Japan alliance is the cornerstone of peace and prosperity in the Asia-Pacific region. We cannot achieve our national goals without a strong partnership between the United States and Japan.

And the alliance between the United States and the Republic of Korea is the lynchpin of stability and security in Northeast Asia. Our alliance with South Korea was forged in shared sacrifice in the Korean war, and it continues to anchor security on the peninsula today.

Each alliance relationship rooted in security cooperation has evolved into an increasingly global partnership that helps provide significant benefits for our people and the international community. We cooperate closely on a wide range of issues, including humanitarian assistance, disaster relief, and in dealing with global hotspots. At the same time, the alliances remain focused on the core mission of safeguarding our security. In particular, that means deterrence and defense against the threat posed by North Korea's continued pursuit of nuclear weapons and ballistic missiles. We will continue to stand shoulder to shoulder with our allies in the face of this danger.

In order to achieve the shared goal of peaceful denuclearization on the Korean Peninsula, we will continue closely to coordinate with the ROK and Japan, as well as with other partners in the region, such as China.

And I want to make very clear that our alliances in Northeast Asia and around the region are not aimed at China. The United States welcomes the rise of a stable and prosperous China which plays a greater role in strengthening regional stability, prosperity, and international rules and norms. Tangible, practical, and visible cooperation between the United States and China is critical to addressing regional and global challenges, from North Korea to climate change. Similarly, the United States seeks good relations between China and its neighbors. We encourage all our allies to pursue positive and constructive relations with China.

We are concerned, however, by an increase in risky and tension-raising activities by China in the East China Sea near the Senkaku Islands, including China's uncoordinated announcement of an Air Defense Identification Zone there. These concerns are amplified by China's behavior in the South China Sea. We will continue to discuss these issues directly with China and with affected countries in the region.

Mr. Chairman, strategic cooperation among the United States, Japan, and the Republic of Korea is essential to the well-being of all our countries in the region. In light of this fact, the current friction between our Japanese and Korean allies is a cause for concern and a problem that requires dedicated efforts by all parties.

In closing, let me make one final point. Bipartisan congressional support for our alliances and the close cooperation between the legislative branches of our three countries have been critical to the success we have achieved over the last six decades, and will be even more important in the future.

So, thank you for inviting me to testify on this important topic. We will hear now from my colleague, but then I am happy to answer any questions that you may have.

[The prepared statement of Mr. Russel follows:]

PREPARED STATEMENT OF HON. DANIEL R. RUSSEL

Chairman Cardin and members of the subcommittee, I am pleased to appear before you today to discuss this important topic.

Early in his first term, President Obama began implementing his vision for the Asia-Pacific rebalance, based on America's enduring stake in a prosperous and stable region. The United States has been, we are, and we will remain a Pacific power. In the second term, the administration is building out this strategy. The Department of State is focused on dedicating diplomatic, public diplomacy, and assistance resources to the region in a way that is commensurate with the truly comprehensive nature of our engagement. And under Secretary Kerry we are intensifying our support for U.S. companies, climate and energy cooperation, people-to-people exchanges, youth and exchange programs, education, women's empowerment, and other initiatives.

The members of this subcommittee know well the importance of the Asia-Pacific region to American interests. The broader region boasts over half the world's population, half of the world's GDP, and nearly half of the world's trade, and is home to some of the world's fastest-growing economies. More and more American citizens are now living, working, and studying in the Asia-Pacific region; people-to-people and family ties have witnessed tremendous growth. Growing numbers of American companies are investing in and exporting products and services to rapidly expanding East Asian markets. And, as the region's economies continue to grow and their interests expand, it becomes increasingly important that the governments and institutions there contribute to upholding and strengthening international law and standards—ranging from human rights to environmental protection to responsible policies on climate change, maritime security, and trade and investment. Simply put, the effects of what happens in the Asia-Pacific region will be felt across the globe and have direct implications for America's interests.

For all of the changes in Asia, this much is constant: our alliances in the region have been and will remain the foundation of our strategy toward the Asia-Pacific. I want to thank you, Mr. Chairman, as well as Ranking Member Rubio and the other members of the subcommittee for your leadership, travel, and public statements which have all underscored the importance of our alliances to our vision of a secure, stable, and prosperous Asia-Pacific region. As you have noted, shared values and a shared history of successful partnership with the United States place Japan and the Republic of Korea (ROK) at the center of this administration's rebalance strategy. The success stories of the ROK and Japan are powerful reminders of the broad range of benefits that accrue from a sustained commitment to free markets, democracy, and close cooperation with the United States. Our alliances with the ROK and Japan contribute significantly to expanded security, stability, and prosperity across the region.

I am pleased to report today that our ties with both countries have never been stronger. Polling shows that the U.S.–ROK relationship enjoys record levels of favorability in South Korea—and the United States has enjoyed this high level of support for the last 2 years. Polling also shows that 84 percent of Japanese citizens support our bilateral alliance. But we do not take our allies for granted. We are working hard with our Japanese and South Korean partners to adjust our presence and to modernize our alliances to help maintain peace and security and address broader shared interests across the Asia-Pacific and around the globe. The upcoming visit by President Obama to Japan and the ROK will propel our efforts.

U.S.-JAPAN ALLIANCE

Let me begin with Japan. The U.S.-Japan alliance is the cornerstone of peace and prosperity in the Asia-Pacific region; we cannot achieve the President's goals without strong and growing ties between the United States and Japan. Our two countries are coordinating closely on a wide range of issues, including regional security and global hotspots. As Secretary Kerry and Foreign Minister Kishida emphasized during their meeting in Washington last month, we are working diplomatically and militarily to strengthen and modernize the U.S.-Japan alliance.

I cannot overstate the importance of our alliance with Japan to continued U.S. leadership in the Asia-Pacific. Over 50,000 U.S. military and civilian personnel are stationed in Japan under the U.S.-Japan security treaty and the U.S.-Japan Status of Forces Agreement, under which Japan provides facilities and areas for U.S. forces for the security of Japan and the maintenance of international peace and security. The Japanese Government provides over $2 billion annually to offset the cost of stationing U.S. forces in Japan: including the USS George *Washington*, which is the only U.S. aircraft carrier in the world that is forward-deployed. This strategic posture means that U.S. forces in Japan are capable of carrying out missions throughout the region and beyond.

U.S. support for the Japan Self-Defense Forces' humanitarian assistance operations in the wake of the 2011 earthquake and tsunami were demonstrations of the alliance's strength and capability and set the stage for U.S.-Japan coordination on Typhoon Haiyan relief in the Philippines in 2013. The unprecedented landing of a U.S. Marine Corps MV–22 Osprey on a Japanese ship during the Haiyan response demonstrated our joint capabilities, and highlighted the interoperability of the U.S. and Japanese militaries.

Our security relationship with Japan made remarkable progress in 2013. Two important successes that my colleague from the Department of Defense can discuss in further detail were the October 2013 "2+2" meeting between Secretaries Kerry and Hagel and their Japanese counterparts, which launched the review of our two countries' Bilateral Defense Guidelines, and Okinawa Governor Nakaima's signing of the landfill permit for the Futenma Relocation Facility. We hope to use the Defense Guidelines review process to modernize our respective roles, missions, and capabilities for an alliance truly capable of meeting the challenges of the 21st century.

Another key development is the Japanese Government's review of what the U.N. Charter describes as, "the right of collective self-defense." Collective self-defense is simply defined as one nation taking action to help defend another nation from attack by a third party.

Japan's Constitution is the only one in the world that explicitly renounces war as an instrument of foreign policy. In the past, Japanese Governments have chosen to interpret their constitution as not permitting the exercise of this right to collective self-defense. It is my understanding that the Japanese Government is studying this interpretation.

The practical effect of a decision by Japan that it would be permissible to conduct collective self-defense could include enabling its U.N. peacekeeping troops to defend other U.N. peacekeepers under attack. Under the current policy, if North Korea were to launch a ballistic missile toward the United States, Japan could not use its ballistic missile defense interceptors to destroy that missile in flight. We recognize this is a decision for the Japanese Government and people, and we welcome Japan's openness and its steps to consult with countries in the region about these deliberations.

U.S.-REPUBLIC OF KOREA ALLIANCE

The U.S.-Republic of Korea alliance is the linchpin of stability and security in Northeast Asia. 2013 marked the 60th anniversary of the U.S.-ROK Mutual Defense Treaty, which serves as the foundation of our alliance and a force for peace and stability on the Korean Peninsula and in Northeast Asia. Our alliance with the ROK was forged in shared sacrifice in the Korean war, and it continues to anchor security in the region today.

As Secretary Kerry reaffirmed during his meetings with ROK leaders in Seoul last month, the U.S.–ROK alliance is a critical component of Washington's strategic engagement with the Asia-Pacific. Our open societies, our shared commitment to democracy and a market economy, and our sustained partnership provide a foundation for the enduring friendship that tightly binds the American and Korean peoples. Over the past six decades, our close cooperation has evolved into an increasingly global partnership, encompassing political, economic, social, and cultural cooperation and providing prosperity for both our peoples.

The United States remains dedicated to the defense of the Republic of Korea, including through extended deterrence and the full range of U.S. military capabilities, both conventional and nuclear, as emphasized in the Joint Declaration issued by President Obama and President Park in May 2013.

The United States and the ROK recently concluded negotiations on a Special Measures Agreement (SMA), by which South Korea will increase its contributions to help offset the cost of stationing of U.S. troops on the Korean Peninsula to $867 million in this year alone, demonstrating that both nations are politically and economically committed to making our alliance more sustainable and adaptable.

We are constantly working to improve readiness and interoperability in order to meet existing and emerging security threats. As my colleague Deputy Assistant Secretary Helvey can describe in detail, last week the United States and the ROK began two of our largest annual joint military exercises, KEY RESOLVE and FOAL EAGLE. Another major annual military exercise, ULCHI FREEDOM GUARDIAN, is scheduled for August. And even as our alliance continues to counter the threat from North Korea, we are expanding our cooperation to meet 21st century challenges beyond the Korean Peninsula.

DPRK-RELATED TENSIONS

Our alliances with the ROK and Japan provide deterrence and defense against the threat posed by the Democratic People's Republic of Korea's (DPRK) continued pursuit of nuclear weapons and ballistic missile technology. We will continue to stand shoulder-to-shoulder with our allies in the face of this growing North Korean threat.

Mr. Chairman, over the years we have seen a pattern of North Korean provocations followed by ''charm offensives'' aimed at extracting payoffs and concessions from the West. Despite the DPRK's recent overtures at engagement, we have yet to see credible indications that North Korea is prepared to come into compliance with the relevant U.N. Security Council resolutions, or even negotiate on the key issue: denuclearization. The United States remains committed to authentic and credible negotiations to implement the September 2005 Joint Statement of the Six-Party Talks and to bring North Korea into compliance with its international obligations through irreversible steps leading to denuclearization. We will not accept North Korea as a nuclear-armed state. We will not reward the DPRK merely for returning to dialogue. As the President has said, the DPRK can achieve the security, respect, and prosperity it claims to seek by choosing the path of denuclearization. For our part, the United States pledges to continue working toward a world in which the people of North and South Korea are peacefully reunited, and the Korean Peninsula is democratic, prosperous, and free of nuclear weapons.

In addition to our concern about the security situation on the Korean Peninsula, the United States remains gravely concerned about the human rights situation in the DPRK. The U.N. Human Rights Council's Commission of Inquiry released its report last month, documenting the deplorable human rights situation in the DPRK. We are working tirelessly to persuade the DPRK Government to release Kenneth Bae, the U.S. citizen who has been held in North Korea for more than a year. We welcome the recent release of an Australian citizen, but continue to urge the DPRK Government to release the ROK citizen still under detention, just as we seek resolution of the cases of the many ROK, Japanese, and other citizens abducted and held by North Korea over the decades.

CHALLENGES: REGIONAL TENSIONS

Mr. Chairman, the United States takes a clear position with regard to behavior of states in connection with their territorial or maritime disputes: we firmly oppose intimidation, coercion, and the use of force. In the East China Sea, we are concerned by an unprecedented increase in risky activity by China's maritime agencies near the Senkaku Islands. The United States returned administration of the Senkakus to Japan in 1972, and they fall within the scope of the U.S.-Japan mutual defense treaty, in particular its Article V. Tensions over the Senkakus have led to a sharp downturn in Sino-Japanese relations. China and Japan are the world's second- and third-largest economies and have a shared interest in a stable environment to facilitate economic prosperity. Neither of these two important countries, nor the global economy, can afford confrontation and crisis.

We object to unilateral actions that seek to change the status quo or advance a territorial claim though extra-legal or nondiplomatic means. Unilateral attempts to change the status quo raise tensions and do nothing under international law to strengthen claims. Therefore we were also concerned by China's sudden and uncoordinated announcement of the Air Defense Identification Zone (ADIZ) over the East China Sea last November. One of the problems with the Chinese ADIZ announcement is that it purports to cover areas administered or claimed by Japan and the ROK. We have been clear that China should not attempt to implement or enforce the ADIZ and it should refrain from taking similar actions in other sensitive or disputed areas.

I do not believe that any party seeks armed conflict in the East China Sea, but unintended incidents or accidents may lead to an escalation of tensions or a tit-for-tat exchange that could escalate. As such, we wholeheartedly endorse calls for crisis-prevention mechanisms, including senior-level communications to defuse situations before they become full-blown crises.

Our concerns are amplified by the situation in the South China Sea, where we are seeing a similar pattern of coercive behavior, strident rhetoric, and ambiguous claims. This is an issue that senior administration officials have raised directly and candidly with Chinese leaders.

I would like to underscore for the committee that the Obama administration has consistently made best efforts to build a strong and cooperative relationship with China. Tangible, practical, and visible cooperation between the United States and China is critical to addressing regional and global challenges, from North Korea to climate change. Similarly, the United States seeks good relations between China and its neighbors; we encourage all our allies to pursue positive and constructive relations with China. I want to make very clear that our alliances, in Northeast Asia and around the region, are not aimed at China.

The United States welcomes the rise of a stable and prosperous China which plays a greater role in strengthening regional stability, prosperity, and international rules and norms. A strong diplomatic, economic, and military presence by the United States has helped create the conditions that made China's extraordinary growth possible and that presence remains essential to regional stability. No country should doubt the resolve of the United States in meeting our security commitments or our determination to uphold the principle of freedom of navigation and overflight. But neither should there be any doubt about the administration's desire for constructive relationship with China based on solving regional and global problems as well as managing disagreement and areas of competition.

STRATEGIC COOPERATION IN THE REGION AND BEYOND

One of the strongest signs of the maturity of our partnerships with the ROK and Japan is our cooperation on global issues beyond our respective borders, from humanitarian assistance to climate change. The benefits of our cooperation with Japan and South Korea are not limited to the people of our three countries, but increasingly accrue to citizens around the world.

Yet at this moment, and despite our many areas of cooperation and common interest, relations between Japan and the Republic of Korea are strained. The current tension between our two allies is a cause for concern, and a problem that requires sincere efforts by both parties to address. There is an urgent need to show prudence and restraint in dealing with difficult historical issues. It is important to handle them in a way that promotes healing. We are working closely with our Japanese and ROK partners to encourage them to take the steps needed to resolve tensions caused by the legacy of the last century through patient and persistent diplomacy. The simple fact, Mr. Chairman, is that strategic cooperation among the United States, Japan, and the ROK is essential to developing the security order in Northeast Asia, especially given the threats facing us and our allies from North Korea and other regional uncertainties. No one can afford to allow the burdens of history to prevent us from building a secure future.

That is why it is so important that we have been able to cooperate with Japan and the ROK on relief efforts, development, and other important projects throughout Southeast Asia. For example, we saw the benefits of increased trilateral disaster response capacity just last fall when the United States, Japan, and South Korea were leading contributors of humanitarian and recovery assistance to the Philippines following the devastation left by Typhoon Haiyan. We are working trilaterally with the ROK and Japan to further improve our interoperability and information sharing during a disaster.

Japan and South Korea are models for other nations in the region and around the world. Both the ROK and Japan have transitioned from one-time recipients of foreign aid to important donors. Whereas once Peace Corps Volunteers were seen throughout the ROK, the Peace Corps and its counterpart recently signed a memorandum of understanding that will enable both parties to cooperate in third countries around the world—in fact, the ROK's Peace Corps counterpart is now the world's second-largest after our own Peace Corps. Last December, during Vice President Biden's visit, the United States and Japan announced the initiation of a U.S.-Japan Development Dialogue between our respective foreign assistance and foreign affairs agencies. The first formal meeting of that dialogue took place last month in Washington.

The Republic of Korea and Japan have been active supporters of international efforts to resolve the Iranian nuclear issue. We are working together on Syria, where Japan and the ROK are providing assistance to address the humanitarian needs of the Syrian people and where both have strongly supported international efforts to find a political solution. U.S. and ROK soldiers have served side by side in Afghanistan, where the Republic of Korea and Japan are major donors to reconstruction and stabilization efforts. Japan has provided over $1.35 billion in assistance to the Palestinians since the mid-1990s, making Japan one of the major donors to the Palestinians after the United States. Our cooperative partnerships with Japan and the Republic of Korea enable increased engagement and impact on a global scale. Both Japan and the ROK are invaluable partners on the international stage, as well; both currently promote our shared values while serving on the U.N. Human Rights Council, and this year the ROK will complete a successful term on the U.N. Security Council.

ALLIANCE TIES

Our deep economic and trade ties with Japan and the ROK provide practical benefits, jobs, and lower consumer prices to Americans. To reap the full reward of our alliance partnerships, we are working to further strengthen our economic relationships and harness the dynamism of growth in the Asia-Pacific region for the benefit of the American people.

The revitalization of Japan's huge economy is of direct interest to the United States. An economically vibrant Japan will attract more U.S. exports, help stimulate even greater Japanese investment in the United States, and serve as a model and source of growth across the Asia-Pacific region. Economic growth will also strengthen Japan as an important partner. We support Japan's goal of unlocking greater growth through structural and regulatory reforms and are working with the private sector as well as Japanese counterparts to bring out the best ideas and solutions to this end. We are also working with Japan to increase economic opportunities for women, both in our own economies and globally. Japanese companies account for approximately 650,000 jobs in the United States, and the United States is one of the largest sources of foreign investment in Japan. Our relationship will continue to grow closer in response to changes such as the availability of U.S. oil and gas to the international market, further integration in high-tech manufacturing, and mutual support for innovative enterprise.

The Republic of Korea is Asia's fourth-largest economy, our sixth-largest goods trading partner, and our fifth-largest export market for agricultural goods. Our two countries have one of the most vibrant trading relationships in the world. Two years since the U.S.-Korea Free Trade Agreement (KORUS FTA) entered into force, our bilateral trade in goods now tops $100 billion annually. During 2012 and 2013, the U.S. enjoyed a $4.4 billion foreign direct investment surplus with Korea. That positive trend looks likely to continue, with recent developments including Hankook Tire's announcement that it plans to invest $800 million to build its first U.S. production plant in Clarksville, TN. The United States is the top destination for ROK foreign direct investment, and Hyundai, Kia, and Samsung now employ thousands of U.S. workers. We are working closely with the Republic of Korea to ensure it fully implements both the letter and spirit of its KORUS commitments, in order to be able to realize the full strategic and economic benefits of the FTA.

As Secretary Kerry noted recently, "A shared commitment to economic growth and innovation is part of why the Trans-Pacific Partnership (TPP) agreement is a cornerstone of the President's economic policy in Asia." That's why one of our highest economic priorities in the region is the successful completion of the TPP negotiations. In the United States, Japan, and other member nations, the TPP will support jobs, foster new business opportunities, and promote economic growth. The TPP will serve as a platform for building a high-standard trade and investment framework for the Asia-Pacific region—promoting transparency, openness, and innovation. Given close trade ties and the strategic importance of closer economic cooperation with our allies, we naturally welcome the ROK's expression of interest in joining the TPP.

Underpinning the historic success of our alliances and our hopes for the future are the robust people-to-people ties between citizens of the United States and citizens of Japan and South Korea. They form the foundation of our partnerships with both countries, helping us to understand and appreciate each other.

Our people-to-people ties with the ROK are dynamic and strong. The ROK sent over 70,000 young people to study in the United States last year—more per capita than any other major sending country—and the number of U.S. students going to the ROK continues to rise. Continuing the trend of U.S.–ROK innovation and investment in educational exchange, last October our countries renewed the Work, English, Study, and Travel (WEST) program, which provides opportunities for qualified university students and recent graduates from the ROK to study English, participate in internships, and travel independently in the United States. ROK students contribute over $2 billion to the U.S. economy; even more important than the immediate economic boost these students bring is the intangible long-term investment in our alliance—a shared experience that underscores to younger generations the enduring value of our partnership.

The Japanese Government has made educational internationalization a component of its growth strategy, and both our governments are working with the private sector, academia, and NGOs to expand mutual understanding and friendship between our young people. While the number of Japanese students earning credit at higher education institutions in the United States has dropped sharply over the last decade, the United States and Japan are committed to increasing two-way student exchange, and both countries have already taken steps—such as increasing grants for study abroad and demystifying the U.S. visa process—that we hope will reverse this trend. We remain dedicated to working with Japan to double student and youth exchanges by 2020 to ensure that our partnership remains strong for decades to come.

I want to make a special note, Mr. Chairman, of acknowledging the Americans in uniform who are currently serving, or have served, in Korea and Japan. Our strong relations with Japan and the ROK would not be possible without the hundreds of thousands of men and women in uniform who have dedicated themselves in the service of our strategic alliances. These service men and women represent the best of the United States in Japan, the ROK, and around the Asia-Pacific region, and upon their return to the United States, they continue to serve as grassroots ambassadors for the great friendship between the United States and our allies.

CONCLUSION

Our alliances with Japan and the ROK are rooted in shared strategic interests in the Asia-Pacific region and around the world, our deep economic ties, and, most importantly, our shared values and the strong personal relationships that have developed through extensive people-to-people ties. Our alliances have never been stronger, and the United States is actively working to deepen our engagement with both countries.

In closing, let me make one final point. Strong, enduring, bipartisan congressional support for our alliances and the close cooperation between the legislative branches of our three countries have been critical to the success we have achieved over the last six decades, and will be even more important in the future.

Senator CARDIN. Thank you very much.
Mr. Helvey.

STATEMENT OF DAVID F. HELVEY, DEPUTY ASSISTANT SECRETARY OF DEFENSE FOR EAST ASIA, U.S. DEPARTMENT OF DEFENSE, WASHINGTON, DC

Mr. HELVEY. Thank you, Mr. Chairman. Thank you for the opportunity to appear today to offer perspectives from the Department of Defense on our alliances in Northeast Asia.

Our treaty alliances and other partnerships remain the foundation for protecting our interests and achieving our security objectives in the Asia-Pacific region, which is why the modernization and continued transformation of these critical relationships forms a central pillar of President Obama's strategy to rebalance to the Asia-Pacific.

Our treaty alliances in Northeast Asia with Japan and the Republic of Korea support this strategy through contributing to a secure and prosperous region, facilitating a defense posture that is geographically distributed, operationally resilient, and politically sustainable, investing in interoperability and strengthening our regional defense cooperation to promote shared interests and advance international rules and norms.

I am pleased to have the opportunity, again, to meet today, and I commend the committee's continued interest in this important subject.

Mr. Chairman, transforming our alliances and partnerships to meet the challenges of the 21st century is the central driver of our efforts with both Japan and the Republic of Korea. We have developed for each alliance a forward-looking agenda based on enhancing security, increasing the ability of our militaries to work together seamlessly, and building our allies' capacity to contribute to regional and global security.

Our alliance with Japan remains the cornerstone of peace and security in the Asia-Pacific region. In October, Secretary Hagel joined Secretary Kerry and their Japanese counterparts in Tokyo for a historic U.S.-Japan Security Consultative Committee meeting that reconfirmed the alliance's commitment to the security of Japan through the full range of U.S. military capabilities, and that set forth a strategic vision reflecting our shared values to promote peace, security, stability, and economic prosperity in the Asia-Pacific.

As part of these efforts, we will be revising our bilateral guidelines for defense cooperation for the first time since 1997, updating our alliance roles and missions, and incorporating new areas of cooperation, such as space and cyber defense. The revision of the guidelines, which we hope to complete by the end of 2014, will ensure that our alliance is capable of responding to the 21st-century challenges. And I can point to the unprecedented landing of the U.S. Marine Corps MV–22 Osprey on a Japanese ship during the Haiyan response, demonstrating the interoperability of the United States and Japanese militaries and our ability to work jointly, as an example of what lies ahead.

We are also taking steps to ensure that our forward military presence in Japan is sustainable over the long term. In December 2013, the Governor of Okinawa approved the Government of Japan's request for a landfill permit necessary to construct a new airfield at Camp Schwab to replace Marine Corps Air Station

Futenma. This was a major step forward. Closing Marine Corps Air Station Futenma and returning other U.S. facilities and areas in Okinawa is central to our plans to reduce the Marine Corps presence on Okinawa by about 9,000 and establish a Marine air-ground task force of about 5,000 marines on Guam. We are delighted that this effort is now on track, and we are confident that the ultimate result will be one that is good for the United States, good for the United States-Japan alliance, and good for the people of Okinawa.

Finally, Japan is one of our most significant ballistic-missile defense partners. Japan is codeveloping the SM–3 Block IIA. It hosts the U.S. Navy's Seventh Fleet. It operates its own BMD-capable Aegis ships, and has agreed to host a second ballistic missile defense radar, in addition to the radar that is already located in Shariki. We hope to have the second radar operational by the end of2014.

Turning to the Republic of Korea, our alliance with the Republic of Korea continues to serve as a lynchpin of peace and stability in the region, and is evolving into a partnership that contributes to security across the globe. Last year, we celebrated the 60th anniversary of the United States-Republic of Korea alliance, welcomed President Park's first year in office, and stood shoulder to shoulder in the face of North Korean provocation.

In October, Secretary Hagel met with Minister Kim for the 45th security consultative meeting in Seoul, a meeting which reaffirmed our bilateral commitment to build a comprehensive strategic alliance based on common values and mutual trust, as well as our two nations' commitment to defend the Republic of Korea through a robust combined defense posture.

In light of the continued threat posed by North Korea, we are taking a number of steps to enhance our force posture and capabilities on the Korean Peninsula so that our combined forces can continue to deter and, if necessary, respond to North Korean aggression or provocation.

Mr. Chairman, the dynamic nature of the region, and the growing threat from North Korea, make trilateral cooperation among the United States, the Republic of Korea, and Japan more important than ever. Simply put, trilateral security cooperation is an essential element of deterrence against North Korean threats. The Department of Defense encourages a healthy and open United States, Republic of Korea, and Japan relationship. To that end, we will continue to look for opportunities for our three countries to exercise together and to use the defense trilateral talks to promote cooperation, dialogue, and transparency between Tokyo and Seoul.

Let me turn briefly to offer some perspectives on another important relationship, the relationship with China. China's economic dynamism, regional influence, and comprehensive military modernization present both opportunities and challenges for the United States-China relationship. We seek a constructive and productive United States-China relationship in which we will pursue opportunities to engage where there is mutual benefit while managing differences in areas of competition.

Within the Department of Defense, we seek to build a United States-China military-to-military relationship that is healthy, stable, reliable, and continuous and supports—and serves as an important part of the overall bilateral relationship. However, we remain concerned about the lack of transparency regarding China's growing military and its increasingly assertive stance on territorial and maritime disputes. We encourage all parties, including China, to deal with their disputes peacefully, without coercion or the use or threat of force, and to ensure that the maritime claims are resolved in accordance with international law. A first step is peacefully addressing these disputes would be to quickly reach agreement with ASEAN on a meaningful code of conduct for the South China Sea.

Mr. Chairman, the Department of Defense will continue to prioritize the Asia-Pacific region, particularly our cooperation with our allies in Northeast Asia. We remain steadfast in our defense commitments to both Japan and the Republic of Korea, and we will continue to work to improve security cooperation, enhance military capabilities, and modernize each of these critical alliances. We look forward to continued support of this committee as we continue to rebalance toward the Asia-Pacific.

Thank you, sir.

[The prepared statement of Mr. Helvey follows:]

PREPARED STATEMENT OF DAVID F. HELVEY

Mr. Chairman and distinguished members of the committee, thank you for the opportunity to appear before you today to offer perspectives from the Department of Defense on efforts to strengthen and transform our alliances in Northeast Asia.

Our treaty alliances and partnerships remain the foundation for protecting our interests and achieving our security objectives in the Asia-Pacific region, which is why the modernization and continued transformation of these critical relationships forms a central pillar of President Obama's strategy to Rebalance to the Asia-Pacific. Our treaty alliances in Northeast Asia—with both Japan and the Republic of Korea (ROK)—contribute directly to this strategy, principally through their contributions to promote a secure and prosperous region; to facilitate the enhancement of a geographically distributed, operationally resilient, and politically sustainable defense posture in the region; to strengthen our readiness through updates to our operational concepts and plans; to invest in interoperable capabilities that are most relevant to the future security environment; and, to strengthen regional defense cooperation in a way that promotes shared interests and that advances international rules and norms. I am pleased to have the opportunity to describe how our alliances help meet these objectives and I commend the committee's continued interest in this important subject.

Mr. Chairman, we are actively working with Japan and the ROK to transform and modernize our alliances in ways that ensure they meet our original security goals of assurance and deterrence while also building our alliances into platforms for broader cooperation on traditional and nontraditional security challenges, both in Asia and globally. In fact, transforming our alliances and partnerships to meet the challenges of the 21st century is the central driver of our efforts with both Japan and the Republic of Korea. In recent years, and in concert with the senior leaders of both countries, we have developed for each alliance a forward-looking agenda based on enhancing security, increasing the ability of our militaries to work together seamlessly, and building our allies' capacity to contribute to regional and global security.

Our alliance with Japan remains the cornerstone of peace and security in the Asia-Pacific region. In October, Secretary Hagel joined Secretary Kerry in Tokyo for the U.S.-Japan Security Consultative Committee (SCC), or 2+2, a historic meeting that marked the first time Japan has hosted this bilateral meeting for the Secretary of Defense and Secretary of State to meet with both of their counterparts. That meeting reaffirmed the indispensable role our two countries play in the maintenance of international peace and security, reconfirmed our alliance's commitment to the security of Japan through the full range of U.S. military capabilities, and set forth a strategic vision that, reflecting our shared values of democracy, the rule of law, free and open markets, and respect for human rights, will effectively promote peace, security, stability, and economic prosperity in the Asia-Pacific region. As part of our efforts to strengthen this critical partnership, we will be revising our bilateral Guidelines for Defense Cooperation for the first time since 1997, updating alliance roles and missions in peacetime and during contingencies to reflect the contemporary security environment, and incorporating new areas of cooperation such as space and cyber defense. This revision of the Guidelines, which we hope to complete by the end of 2014, will ensure that our alliance is capable of responding to 21st century challenges.

In addition to updating alliance roles and missions, we are taking steps to ensure that our forward military presence in Japan is sustainable over the long term. Critical to this effort is our plan for the realignment of U.S. Marine Corps forces on Okinawa. In December 2013, Governor Nakaima of Okinawa approved the Government of Japan's request for a landfill permit necessary to construct a new airfield at Camp Schwab to replace Marine Corps Air Station Futenma. This was a major step forward, and is testament to the strong leadership and commitment to the alliance on the part of Prime Minister Abe. Closing MCAS Futenma and returning other U.S. facilities and areas in Okinawa—approximately 2,500 acres of land—is central to our plans to reduce the Marine Corps presence on Okinawa by about 9,000 and establish a Marine Air Ground Task Force of about 5,000 Marines on Guam.

When this effort is complete, we will have operational Marine Air-Ground Task Forces in multiple locations across the theater, increasing our ability to respond quickly to regional crises and contingencies. The remaining Marines on Okinawa will be more concentrated in less populated parts of the island, and centered on a new air station that the Government of Japan will build. This realignment and movement of troops to Guam advances our goal of having a geographically distributed, operationally resilient, and politically sustainable force presence in the region. We are delighted that this effort is now on-track, and are confident that the ultimate result will be one that is good for the United States, for the U.S.-Japan Alliance, and for the people of Okinawa.

Finally, it is worth emphasizing that Japan is one of our most significant ballistic missile defense (BMD) partners, as evidenced by our cooperation in codeveloping the next generation sea-based interceptor, the SM–3 Block IIA; its role as host for the U.S. Navy 7th Fleet, and the Japan Maritime Self Defense Force's own BMD-capable Aegis ships; and its agreement to host a second TPY–2 BMD radar, in addition to the radar already located in Shariki. We hope to have the second radar operational by the end of 2014. Japan is truly a model BMD partner, and we look forward to expanding on that cooperation in the future.

Similarly, the U.S.-ROK Alliance continues to serve as a linchpin of peace and stability in the region and is evolving into a partnership that contributes to security across the globe. Last year we celebrated the 60th Anniversary of the U.S.-ROK Alliance, we welcomed President Park's first year in office, and we continued to stand together in the face of North Korean provocation. In October, Secretary Hagel met with Minister Kim in the 45th Security Consultative Meeting (SCM). That meeting reaffirmed our bilateral commitment to build a comprehensive strategic alliance based on common values and mutual trust as well as our two nations' mutual commitment to defend the Republic of Korea through a robust combined defense posture. To enhance effective deterrence options against North Korean nuclear weapons and other weapons of mass destruction (WMD), Secretary Hagel and Minister Kim formally endorsed a bilateral "Tailored Deterrence Strategy" that establishes a strategic alliance framework that strengthens the integration of alliance capabilities to maximize their deterrent effects.

In light of the threats posed by North Korea, we are also taking a number of steps to enhance our force posture and capabilities on the Korean Peninsula. We are especially focused on enhancing the alliance's military capabilities to ensure that our combined forces maintain the defense of the Republic of Korea and can deter and, if necessary, respond to North Korean aggression or provocation. One of our highest priorities is the development of comprehensive alliance countermissile capabilities to detect, defend against, disrupt, and destroy missile threats. This effort includes interoperable intelligence, surveillance, and reconnaissance (ISR) systems and missile defenses, as well as the supporting command, control, communications, and computers (C4).

As part of our work to modernize the alliance, we continually assess progress toward implementation of the Strategic Alliance 2015 (SA 2015) plan in order to ensure continued readiness to provide for the combined defense of the Korean Peninsula after the transition of operational control in wartime to the ROK. A new cost-sharing agreement with the ROK will help ensure that we have the resources necessary for the combined defense and that both countries are sharing in the investment the alliance requires to defend South Korea. We continue to make progress in the development of our bilateral plans, including the completion last

March of the U.S.-ROK Counter-Provocation Plan, which enables our two countries to respond jointly and more effectively to North Korean provocations. We also regularly exercise to ensure the readiness of the Combined Forces Command (CFC). Currently, we are in the middle of the bilateral military exercises KEY RESOLVE and FOAL EAGLE, which are, respectively, an annual command post exercise and an annual series of joint and combined field training exercises.

In addition to advancing our bilateral alliances with Japan and the ROK, the dynamic nature of the region and the growing threat from North Korea make trilateral cooperation among the United States, the ROK, and Japan more important than ever. Simply put, trilateral security cooperation is an essential element of deterrence against North Korean threats. The Department of Defense encourages a healthy and open trilateral relationship in order to facilitate better relations with our two closest allies in Northeast Asia. To that end, we continually look for opportunities for our three countries to participate in military exercises and highly value our Defense Trilateral Talks (DTT) as a forum to promote cooperation, dialogue, and transparency between Tokyo and Seoul.

Let me turn briefly to offer some perspectives from the Department of Defense on another important relationship, the relationship with China.

China's economic dynamism, regional influence, and pursuit of a long-term, comprehensive military modernization program, present both opportunities and challenges for the U.S.-China relationship. Thus, we seek a constructive and productive U.S.-China relationship, in which we will pursue opportunities to engage where there is mutual benefit, while managing differences and areas of competition. Within the Department of Defense, we seek to build a U.S.-China military-to-military relationship that is healthy, stable, reliable, and continuous, and an important part of the overall bilateral relationship. The Department is pursuing three key areas of focus for the military-to-military relationship: (1) sustained, substantive dialogue; (2) concrete, practical cooperation in areas of mutual interest such as counterpiracy, humanitarian assistance and disaster relief, military medicine, and maritime safety; and (3) building risk reduction mechanisms to manage differences responsibly.

However, we remain concerned about a lack of transparency regarding China's growing military and its increasingly assertive behavior in the maritime domain, highlighted by its announcement in November of an Air Defense Identification Zone in the East China Sea and continued pressure against other claimants in the South China Sea based on its ill-defined "9-dash line" claim. We encourage all parties, including China, to reject intimidation, coercion, and aggression and to base their claims on well-founded principles of international law and to pursue them peacefully through diplomatic processes in accordance with international law and norms through the establishment of peaceful, diplomatic processes for preventing maritime conflicts. A good first step would be timely conclusion of a China-ASEAN Code of Conduct for the South China Sea.

Moving forward, as the United States builds a stronger foundation for a military-to-military relationship with China, we will also continue to monitor China's evolving military strategy, doctrine, and force development and encourage China to be more transparent about its military modernization program. In concert with our allies and partners, the Department will continue adapting U.S. forces, posture, and operational concepts to maintain a stable and secure Asia-Pacific security environment.

Mr. Chairman, the Department of Defense will continue to prioritize the Asia-Pacific region, particularly our robust cooperation with allies in Northeast Asia. We remain steadfast in our defense commitments to both Japan and the Republic of Korea and will continue to work to improve security cooperation, enhance military capabilities, and modernize each of these critical alliances. We look forward to the continued support of this committee as we continue to rebalance toward the Asia-Pacific.

Senator CARDIN. Well, thank both of you for your testimony, but, more importantly, thank you for your service during this critically important time.

Mr. Helvey, I want to start with a statement that was made this morning. I understand that it has been somewhat taken back, but I want to make sure that the record is clear here. I am referring to Assistant Secretary of Defense Katrina McFarland talking about the administration's budget as it relates to the Department of Defense. And she said, and I quote, "Right now, the pivot is being looked at again, because, candidly, it cannot happen." That had many of us concerned as to the administration's commitment to the Rebalance to Asia. Can you clarify the current priority within the administration and how this budget will be consistent with that priority?

Mr. HELVEY. Well, sir, there has been a clarification that was issued, and, you know, in brief, the Rebalance to Asia can and will continue. And this is exactly what we have done in the 2015 Defense budget.

The President's decision to rebalance to the Asia-Pacific reflects a careful assessment of the long-term U.S. interest in the peace and prosperity of the Asia-Pacific region, and also reflects the strong and inextricable ties between the United States and other Pacific nations. In this respect, the rebalance is driven by our calculation of our interests rather than determined by the resources.

This is not to say that resources do not count, however. As Secretary Hagel spoke of last week in discussing the 2015 budget which was submitted today, the funding levels we seek provide the opportunity to present a responsible approach that protects readiness and modernization while maintaining a force large enough to fulfill our defense strategy, though with some additional risk. As he said, we have to adapt, innovate, and make difficult decisions. And we have done that in our budget. Our resourcing will enable us to uphold our commitment to the region, including a strengthened posture and presence, and ensure the United States preserves its status as the preeminent military power in the region.

Senator CARDIN. Thank you for that clarification.

Let me just point out, when you look at the regional bureaus and the support that they have received within the Department of State budget and within DOD, Asia, while not at the bottom, is not as strong as it should have been. The last several budgets by the Obama administration have tried to balance that to reflect the priority in Asia. Can we expect that resources will continue to be prioritized toward the Rebalance to Asia?

Mr. HELVEY. Yes, sir, at least from within the Defense budget, our resources do reflect those priorities, as outlined in the Defense Strategic Guidance from 2012. As I said, the budget that we have presented allows us to fulfill our defense strategy, which includes the rebalance toward the Asia-Pacific.

Now, within the Department of Defense, as you know, sir, our budgets are not allocated by region, they are allocated through the services. And so, many of the things that we are doing, whether it is partner-building capacity or cooperation, investing in capabilities that are most relevant to the Asia-Pacific, those are reflected in the budget.

Senator CARDIN. In the Department of State, there are regional allocations. How are we doing, Mr. Russel, with the budget?

Mr. RUSSEL. Well, thank you for asking, Chairman. This is an important priority for all of us, and it is an important priority for President Obama. I know, from my time at the National Security Council, when we conducted an interagency exercise, along with the Office of Management and Budget, to bring together not only the Asia policy people from each of the relevant departments, but also the comptrollers and the budget people, to underscore the priority that President Obama places on the Asia-Pacific as a strategic priority.

In the case of the State Department, as you noted, the Obama administration has made some headway in funding more robustly our Asia-Pacific priorities. And, while Secretary Kerry himself will be testifying before the Senate on the State Department budget next week, and I know, as a matter of practice, it is not good for the Assistant Secretary to get out ahead of the Secretary, I can say, as Deputy Secretary Heather Higginbottom briefed the press earlier today, that the President's fiscal year 2015 budget represents a continuation of the commitment to fully fund the rebalance.

I know that the fiscal year budget, like the FY14 request, the budget for 2015 shows a significant increase in funding for our programs in the Asia-Pacific region. I believe Deputy Secretary Higginbottom pegged that at approximately a 9-percent increase. Moreover, in other areas, including public diplomacy and in the overall utilization and ability to maximize the resources and the personnel that we have in the region, we believe that we have made, and continue to make, headway in intensifying our efforts in fulfilling our national strategy.

Senator CARDIN. Thank you for that. I had not intended to spend time at this hearing on that, but, considering Secretary McFarland's initial comments, I thought it was important that we clarify that. And I expect, next week, when Secretary Kerry is before the full committee on his budget, that we are going to be talking more about Ukraine, Iran, and Syria than we will be able to get into the specifics on the budget, but I do intend to ask questions for the record on some of these issues, and I am pleased to hear your comments, Mr. Russel.

Mr. Helvey, I want to discuss part of your statement on dealing with the Okinawa stationing of marines. This has been a thorn in our relationship for over 15 years. The community certainly has changed dramatically since that military facility was first constructed. It has presented a real PR problem between Japan and the United States. We all recognize that our future alliance requires different locations for facilities, and we have been working on this for a long time. And there have been challenges. There have been challenges in Japan, there have been challenges in Congress, there have been a lot of questions asked, a lot of good questions asked, about the economics of this and whether it works, and whether it works for the future.

So, I am very much interested in your, I guess, summary comment, ''We are delighted that this effort is now on track, and are confident that the ultimate result will be one that is good for the United States, for the United States-Japan alliance, and for the people of Okinawa.''

If you would not mind just expanding a little bit more as to what you think is a realistic time schedule for us to implement the understanding between Japan and the United States.

Mr. HELVEY. Well, sir, thank you for that question. As you pointed out, this is a longstanding issue that we have been working with our colleagues and counterparts in the Government of Japan. Since at least 1996, the United States and Japan have been in agreement on the need to relocate the existing Marine Corps Air

Station at Futenma, around which, as you noted, a significant population has grown in recent years.

Since 1999, we have agreed on a site in the vicinity of Camp Schwab, near the village of Henoko, so I am—this kind of gives you a sense of, you know, the timeline as it has evolved. And this, again, was confirmed most recently last October in the Two-Plus-Two statement that we had with our counterparts—Secretary Hagel and Secretary Kerry, with their counterparts.

So, the agreement by the Governor of Okinawa to approve the landfill permit does reflect a significant step forward, because we are now in a position where the Government of Japan can now begin construction on the airstrip at Camp Schwab to start building out what the Futenma Replacement Facility, as it is known in the vernacular, where that is going to be——

Senator CARDIN. But, let me give you what I——

Mr. HELVEY [continuing]. In 10 to 20 years.

Senator CARDIN. In my visit to Japan, and in my conversations with my colleagues on the Armed Services Committee and on the Appropriations Committee, it seems to me that we do not have a clear understanding as to the sequencing of appropriations in Japan and the United States to make this a reality. Are you confident that we have an understanding with the Government of Japan as to how their Parliament will be funding the staging and funding the new facilities that are necessary for this transition, consistent with the ability of Congress to also appropriate the funds necessary for the transition to Guam and Hawaii?

Mr. HELVEY. Senator, I would like to take that question for the record, if I could. I am going to have to do some additional consultations to be able to provide a fulsome response.

[EDITOR'S NOTE.—The requested information can be found in the Q&A in the "Additional Material Submitted for the Record" at the end of this hearing.]

Senator CARDIN. And I appreciate that. I want to make sure things are accurate.

I just think it is important that we have clear understandings, and there has been a reluctancy in Congress to do certain things as it is still unclear what is being done in Japan. And I think it is important that, if we are all sincere, we are trying to move forward with this relocation, which is absolutely essential, that we have a transparent and an open strategy with Japan as to the viability of the projects, to make sure that we have accurate funding dollar amounts, and that there is a commitment to fund it in a timely way by both Parliaments, in the United States and in Japan.

Let me move forward to Korea and talk a little bit about the transition of authority on the troops there, as the OPCON is supposed to be implemented in December 2015. How are we doing in regards to the implementation of that commitment to turn over command to the Koreans?

Mr. HELVEY. Well, Senator Cardin, the transition of wartime operational control, which is the central point of your question, should sustain and enhance the alliance's combined defense posture and capabilities, support both the alliance's bilateral defense priorities and its future development. The United States and the

Republic of Korea remain committed to making the preparations necessary to transfer wartime operational control on the timeline that was established in the Strategic Alliance 2015 Plan, which would be December 2015.

OPCON transition, however, has always been conditions-based, and we continue to assess and review the security situation on the Korean Peninsula, in the context of implementation of the Strategic Alliance 2015 Plan. One of the key outcomes from the security consultative meeting last October between Secretary Hagel and Minister Kim was the establishment of an OPCON Working Group, where the United States and the Republic of Korea are examining where we are, in terms of both sides, the United States and the Republic of Korea, in meeting the timelines and the commitments under the Strategic Alliance 2015 Plan, in light of a request from the Republic of Korea to look at the conditions for transition of operational control.

So, we are in the process of doing that. It is something that we do regularly through our alliance. We are meeting the timelines now, but we just want to make sure that we are taking a look at where we are going to be going, in the context of the changing security environment, particularly in North Korea.

Senator CARDIN. Mr. Russel, moving to the relationship between the Republic of Korea and North Korea, and the regional concerns on the activities within North Korea. Obviously what gets most of the attention is their nuclear activities, but there is also the erratic behavior of the government, the way that they treat their own people, and gross violations of human rights, the failure to have an economy that can adequately take care of the needs of their own people, all of which have presented challenges for the international community.

It appears like there is a dialogue taking place between the Republic of Korea and North Korea. Of course, we had the six-party talks. Can you just update us as to the confidence level that we have a method for trying to resolve issues in North Korea?

Mr. RUSSEL. Yes. Thank you, Mr. Chairman.

First and foremost, our approach to North Korea is predicated on very, very close coordination, in the first instance, with our ROK ally, as well as with Japan, and then broader coordination with the other partners in the six-party process and with the international community. The ability of the United States to maintain a united front, and the insistence that North Korea has to come into compliance with its international obligation to begin denuclearizing, is one of the things that has served as a bulwark against now familiar North Korean tactics.

One familiar cycle we have seen in North Korean behavior is generating regional tension through provocative steps and threatening behavior, only to follow that with a so-called ''charm offensive,'' in the hopes that they will be able to elicit concessions and substantive rewards from the United States, from the ROK, and from the international community. They have failed in that effort.

The agreement by North Korea, belatedly, to move forward with the exchange of elderly family members separated by the Korean war, bringing together aged South and North Koreans who have not seen each other, in some cases, for many decades, was a welcome step, but it is a step that we attribute to the Park administration's firm and principled-based approach to dealing with North Korea.

Like the United States, the Government of the Republic of Korea insists that North Korea must take irreversible steps to begin coming into compliance on its denuclearization obligations, that humanitarian actions can be pursued, and the ROK has taken some modest steps in that direction, but there will be no progress until and unless North Korea accepts that its nuclear program and its ballistic missile program are not acceptable to the international community, and directly at odds with North Korea's own stated desire for greater security, as well as economic assistance, if not integration.

Based on this firm set of principles and close coordination between the United States and our allies and our partners, we have denied North Korea consistently the benefits that it had previously achieved through its misbehavior and through its threats.

On human rights, the United States has strongly supported the Human Rights Council's decision to form a Commission of Inquiry, which recently issued a report and will be discussed next month— or later this month, in Geneva, by the Human Rights Council. That report found a truly appalling set of circumstances in North Korea, and was able to document many of the very, very troubling practices there.

The United States will continue to work with the international community and with our partners, including the ROK, to speak out and to shine a light on the problems of human rights in North Korea, even as we focus intently on the requirement that North Korea take steps to denuclearize and to end its illegal ballistic missile program.

Senator CARDIN. Thank you for that answer.

Is there anything new to report in regards to our efforts to improve the relationship between our two close allies, the Republic of Korea and Japan? Have there been any new initiatives? There seems to be some provocative activities; there were provocative activities last year. Do we see any good will that we might be able to foster a better relationship between those two countries?

Mr. RUSSEL. Well, Mr. Chairman, it is very much in the interests of the United States, and therefore it is very much a diplomatic priority for the United States, that the friction and the tension between these two extraordinarily close friends and allies of the United States be reduced, and be reduced quickly. Both Japan and the Republic of Korea need to make respective efforts to help create a more conducive and positive climate. They are both dealing with the legacy of very, very sensitive and very difficult issues, historical issues from the 20th century. We have maintained a direct and candid dialogue with the political and the governmental on the opinion leaders in both countries. We continue to stress the need for prudence and for restraint for all parties to take steps that will promote healing. These legacy issues cannot be solved by any one party, alone. But, all parties can contribute to a reversal of the current atmosphere and the creation of a positive trend.

Both the Republic of Korea and Japan are healthy, stable democracies. They are both important free-market economies. They, themselves, have close cultural ties and roots in shared values. Moreover, both the Republic of Korea and Japan have a huge strategic interest in bilateral, as well as trilateral, cooperation, including and particularly because of the threat posed by North Korea.

The United States and Japan have, I think, set a positive model of how two countries can move from the enmity of war to reconciliation and an extraordinary partnership, friendship, and alliance. That is a model that I hope can increasingly be emulated by other countries. It is necessary to deal with the sensitive issues of history to ensure that that history does not obstruct the ability of Japan and the Republic of Korea to meet the challenges of today and to fulfill the goals of tomorrow.

So, the short answer, after a long introduction, Mr. Chairman, to your question, is, yes, the United States has both an interest and a role, not as a mediator, but as a friend and as a partner. That is a role that we are pursuing with vigor.

Senator CARDIN. Well, I think this has to be a very high priority. We want to see good relations with all the countries in that region of the world. One of my concerns is that it looks like China is trying to increase the wedge between Japan and the Republic of Korea to establish a closer relationship with the Republic of Korea, to the detriment of Japan. It is critically important that the United States, which has close alliances with Japan and Republic of Korea, that we use our relationships to improve the relationship between those two countries.

In my visit last year, it was so obvious. More questions were asked, I think, on that subject than any other subject, even though the maritime security problems were huge and China's huge. But, these historic disputes have caused real challenges to the functioning relationship between two allies of the United States.

With that, I thank our witnesses.

Mr. Helvey, I just want to underscore the importance of trying to get on the same page on the replacements to Okinawa. This is an issue that is critically important to both countries. We support it, but we have to have the numbers that make sense, and we have to be on the same page with, in regards to our mutual commitments. So, I look forward to that information being made available to our committee.

Thank you.

We will now turn to our second panel. And we are pleased to have two distinguished experts on Northeast Asia. First is Dr. Sheila Smith, a senior fellow for Japan Studies at the Council on Foreign Relations. Dr. Smith currently directs the Project on Japan's Political Transition and the U.S.-Japan Alliance.

And then we have Dr. Michael Auslin, a resident scholar and the director of Japan Studies at the American Enterprise Institute, AEI, where he studies Asian regional security and political issues. Mr. Auslin is also a biweekly columnist for the Wall Street Journal.

Welcome, both of you. We look forward to your testimony. As I indicated earlier, your written comments will be made part of our committee record, and you may proceed as you wish.

Dr. Smith.

STATEMENT OF SHEILA SMITH, SENIOR FELLOW FOR JAPAN STUDIES, COUNCIL ON FOREIGN RELATIONS, WASHINGTON, DC

Dr. SMITH. Chairman Cardin, thank you for the privilege of joining you today to discuss our alliances in Northeast Asia.

Japan and the Republic of Korea are two of America's closest allies. Both were forged in the wake of World War II and at the beginning of the cold war that defined the last half of the 20th century. We have over 60 years of shared history in managing regional security in Northeast Asia. We have economic ties that are deepening for the pursuit of new trade agreements and new energy ties. And we share a common interest in the norms and institutions that govern international relations, particularly regarding the peaceful resolution of international disputes. These are close U.S. partnerships, with a burgeoning agenda of cooperation.

Both alliances also face new sources of challenge. The first is the changing strategic balance in Northeast Asia. For over a decade now, the stability of that region has been tested by the proliferation ambitions of North Korea. In addition, the rising influence of China is reshaping the region's diplomatic, economic, and military relationships.

Our bilateral relations with both Japan and South Korea are strong. Last fall, Secretary Hagel traveled to Seoul to mark the 60th anniversary of our security treaty and for the bilateral ROK–U.S. Security Consultative Meeting. From there, he traveled to Tokyo, where he was joined by Secretary Kerry for a Security Consultative Committee "two-plus-two" meeting with their Japanese counterparts. At both meetings, a detailed agenda of alliance cooperation was outlined, with very similar aims of strengthening deterrence and defense cooperation.

In Japan, the Defense reforms initiated by Prime Minister Abe inform our revision of the U.S.-Japan Guidelines for Defense Cooperation. Similarly, we are building strong economic and energy partnerships with Japan and South Korea. The KORUS Trade Agreement has been a tremendous benefit to both South Korea and the United States, and we are working with Japan to complete negotiations on the Trans-Pacific Partnership.

Energy cooperation, I believe, also strengthens our partnership with these Northeast Asian allies. We continue to discuss renewal of our civilian nuclear agreement with Seoul, and we have initiated new LNG projects with Japan.

But, today our biggest challenge may be the deterioration of relations between Seoul and Tokyo. Memories of the past century continue to infuse contemporary political relations in Northeast Asia. And, since 2012, the Japan-ROK relationship has taken a turn for the worse. President Lee Myung-bak's visit to Dokdo, or Takeshima, as the Japanese refer to them, that summer, and the progress of Korean court cases inside South Korea over victims' claims for World War II compensation from Japan have called into question the foundation of postwar Japan-ROK diplomacy.

Popular sentiments in both countries have gone from mutual respect to antagonism. Newly elected leaders in both capitals, President Park Geun-hye and Prime Minister Abe Shinzo, have failed to find a path to overcome their diplomatic estrangement.

Next year will be the 50th anniversary of the Bilateral Peace Treaty that negotiated the basis of postwar reconciliation and restored diplomatic ties between these two U.S. allies. Without high-level dialogue, that anniversary could be an even more difficult moment for the relationship.

This worsening Japan-South Korea relationship comes at a time of considerable change in Northeast Asia. China's rising economic and military influence has had a tremendous effect on both societies, and there, too, the postwar settlement is called into question. Most worrisome is the relationship between Japan and China, who have confronted each other in the waters around the Senkakus as Beijing has sought to contest Japan's administrative control over these remote, uninhabited islands. Chinese paramilitary ships continue to challenge the Japan Coast Guard, and in 2013 the Chinese military began to intimate its interest in the airspace and waters around these islands. The announcement, in November last year, of a new Chinese Air Defense Identification Zone adds another layer of complexity to the already dangerous tensions developing in the East China Sea.

The United States must pursue three priorities in Northeast Asia. First, Washington must continue its crucial role in deterring aggression and in advocating for risk reduction in this increasingly crowded East China Sea maritime space. Second, the United States must do all that it can to encourage the leaders of Japan and South Korea to overcome their political resistance to dialogue. Washington cannot broker reconciliation, but must continue to point out the costs of continued estrangement, for regional stability as well as to their own security.

Finally, the United States must continue to deepen the economic bonds, including energy, that sustain our relations with Japan and South Korea. Our own future well-being and security will depend upon these alliances as we navigate the challenges of a transforming Asia-Pacific.

Thank you very much, and I look forward to your questions.

[The prepared statement of Dr. Smith follows:]

PREPARED STATEMENT OF DR. SHEILA A. SMITH

U.S. alliances in Northeast Asia are critical to the success of our Asia strategy. These alliances are half a century old, with extensive agendas of economic and security cooperation. Japan and South Korea continue to host the bulk of our forward deployed forces in Asia, yet these are not just military alliances. The people of Japan and South Korea share our commitment to democratic values, to an open and fair global trading order, and to a cooperative approach to ensuring regional stability in a rapidly changing Asia-Pacific.

Both Japan and South Korea have new political leaders: in December 2012, Abe Shinzo was elected Prime Minister after his Liberal Democratic Party (LDP) gained a majority in Japan's Lower House of Parliament and Park Geun-hye was elected to a 5-year term as South Korea's President by a wide margin, assuming office in February 2013. Abe's LDP received overwhelming support in the Upper House election of Parliament in the July 2013, giving the conservatives a majority in both Houses of Parliament for the first time since 2007. Park had led her Saenuri Party as it maintained its majority in the April 2012 legislative elections for the National Assembly. Thus both leaders have a strong electoral mandate, and will be in power for the next several years.

Unfortunately, the relationship between Tokyo and Seoul has deteriorated significantly, making it difficult for the United States to deepen and expand cooperation with its allies. Where once strong trilateral cooperation between Washington, Seoul, and Tokyo could be expected across a wide range of issues, today that cooperation is less likely. For over a year now, the leaders of Japan and South Korea have not met.

UPDATE ON U.S.–ROK ALLIANCE

The Republic of Korea continues to face an unstable and unpredictable regime in Pyongyang. Last fall, the United States and the Republic of Korea commemorated the 60th anniversary of their alliance and outlined plans for advancing the emerging global partnership between Washington and Seoul. The U.S.–ROK alliance has successfully deterred aggression by North Korea against the South on the Korean Peninsula. Washington and Seoul work closely to craft and support the U.N. Security Council Resolutions that seek to sanction North Korean proliferation. After successive incidents in 2010 involving the use of force by Pyongyang against the South, the U.S.–ROK alliance has bolstered defense cooperation and strengthened their combined defense posture. In March 2013, the two governments completed their ''counter provocation plan,'' designed to anticipate and meet any further military actions by the North Koreans. In addition, last fall Secretary of Defense Chuck Hagel and Defense Minister Kim Kwan-jin approved a ''tailored deterrence strategy'' that would meet WMD threats from the North, and this includes the counter missile as well as the Korean Air and Missile Defense system.

The U.S.–ROK alliance also includes a global agenda of cooperation. Since 2009, in accordance with the Joint Vision for the alliance, the United States and South Korea have set forth a broader agenda of global cooperation, including partnering in developing mechanisms for ensuring global nuclear security. South Korea hosted the second Nuclear Security summit in 2012. In addition, South Korea continues to expand its peacekeeping, post-conflict reconstruction, and disaster relief activities, and cooperates with the United States and others in Syria and Afghanistan. Future goals for the alliance include achieving the transition of wartime operational control (OPCON), deepening cooperation through their Cyber Cooperation Working Group, and continuing to implement base relocation and returns of U.S. Forces Korea (USFK).

UPDATE ON U.S.-JAPAN ALLIANCE

The U.S.-Japan alliance has also confronted a new security challenge. Since 2012, China has begun maritime patrols of the Senkaku Islands in the East China Sea, challenging Japan's administrative control. Rising tensions, and growing popular sensitivities over the islands, have frozen diplomatic relations between Tokyo and Beijing, and the increasing paramilitary patrols have upon occasion been supplemented by interactions between the two militaries.

The United States has direct interests in this growing tension. As Japan's treaty ally, the United States has increased its defense cooperation with Tokyo (such as the deployment of F–22s in Okinawa and expanded training between U.S. and Japanese forces, including amphibious landing operations) to deter miscalculation, and has conveyed to Beijing in repeated high-level meetings (including between President Barack Obama and Chinese President Xi Jinping last year) the U.S. interest in a peaceful resolution of China's maritime disputes with its neighbors. China's announcement in November 2013 of a new Air Defense Identification Zone (ADIZ) in the East China Sea, however, puts new pressure on Japan's air defenses (as well as South Korea's) and exacerbates tensions over the Senkaku Islands.

The U.S.-Japan alliance has also begun an important set of revisions as Japan has initiated its own defense reforms. In October, Secretary of State John Kerry and Secretary of Defense Hagel traveled to Tokyo for a Security Consultative Committee (2+2) meeting with Foreign Minister Fumio Kishida and Defense Minister Itsunori Onodera. The highlights of that meeting included an agreement to revise the U.S.-Japan Defense Cooperation Guidelines to enhance the alliance deterrent (especially with intelligence, surveillance and reconnaissance (ISR) capabilities). A review of roles, missions, and capabilities will supplement the discussion of the Guidelines, as will a review in Japan of the government's interpretation of the constitution with regard to the right of collective self-defense.

Finally, Japan's economic policy reforms, dubbed ''Abenomics,'' have had some initial success in raising expectations for an improved economic performance. A combination of fiscal stimulus and a new emphasis on monetary policy combined to stimulate greater optimism in Japan's economic future. Breaking the deflationary mindset is seen as the prerequisite to greater investment and consumer spending. Early signs of traction in 2013 were apparent, but much will depend on the Abe government's ability to tackle the more politically difficult economic restructuring Japan needs to truly turn its economy around. Japan's decision last year to join the

Trans-Pacific Partnership (TPP) is widely seen as one of Prime Minister Abe's best policy tools for opening the market and restoring economic competitiveness.

CHALLENGES FOR 2014

The United States has several challenges ahead in managing its alliance relations in Northeast Asia. First, both alliances will need continued attention to defense cooperation. Regional security trends make alliance readiness and strategic adjustments to the alliance deterrent necessary. The United States and Japan will revise their Defense Cooperation Guidelines to consider new missions and upgrade capabilities based on their strategic assessment of regional military balance. Tensions in the East China Sea and the continued concern over the situation on the Korean Peninsula will require continued attention to crisis management provisions and to reassess the alliance readiness. Force posture adjustment continues to be necessary, as are upgrades in alliance deterrence (such as the ongoing improvements in ISR and ballistic missile defense capabilities). Japan's own reorientation of its defense posture southward will also shape alliance cooperation. In the U.S.–ROK alliance, the most important consultations continue to be over whether to transition OPCON from the USFK to the Korean military. The nature and timing of this transfer, of course, will be conditions based, and should be undertaken in order to ensure a seamless combined deterrent force. The potential for provocations from the North cannot be underestimated, especially near the Northern Limit Line (NLL), and close allied consultations on how to anticipate and respond to such provocations remains a high priority. Finally, the potential for intermediate range missile and/or nuclear testing remains, and the continued ability to deter (including extended deterrence) is crucial to regional stability.

Second, economic cooperation continues to be an important component in our alliance cooperation. The TPP negotiations are a critical component of U.S.-Japan cooperation. Recent slowing of progress rests largely on two requirements. The first is that the lack of trade promotion authority prompts concerns over the ability of the Obama administration to gain congressional approval of a final agreement. Second, the desire for a high standards agreement limits the U.S. willingness for compromise, particularly on Japanese agriculture. Domestic politics in both countries could undercut the U.S.-Japan cooperation that to date had enabled progress on this important economic security initiative. The United States and South Korea now enjoy the benefits of their free trade agreement (KORUS), approved by the U.S. Congress and the Korean Assembly at the end of 2011. Differences remain over some sectors, but overall trade has improved.

Finally, energy cooperation will also be on the alliance agenda this year, and with both allies, energy has a strategic impact. The United States and South Korea will continue to discuss their civilian nuclear cooperation, and expectations remain high that a new agreement can be reached. Additional time was granted by the Senate in January 2014 to allow a more careful discussion. Japan too has new energy needs after its triple disasters in 2011 changed the national consensus on the country's overall energy mix. Exports of U.S. liquefied natural gas (LNG) and potentially other energy resources to Japan should be considered, as they will transform Japan's dependence on Russia and the Middle East for the bulk of its imported energy needs.

BILATERAL COOPERATION BETWEEN TOKYO AND SEOUL

Perhaps the thorniest issue for U.S. foreign policy in Northeast Asia continues to be the difficult relations between Seoul and Tokyo. Since coming into office, President Park and Prime Minister Abe have failed to organize a high-level summit meeting, and as a result, domestic sentiments within each country have become increasingly antagonistic. Several factors account for the deterioration in this important bilateral relationship. First, the continuing sensitivity particularly in South Korea to issues related to historical memory impedes closer security cooperation. In 2012, the two nations were close to concluding two important security agreements, an information-sharing agreement and an acquisitions and cross-servicing agrement (ACSA) that would have allowed cooperation in case of a contingency on the peninsula. Domestic politics in South Korea derailed this effort, however.

Second, the visit in 2012 of former Korean President Lee Myung-bak to the island of Dokdo (Takeshima for the Japanese) inflamed popular sentiment in Japan, as did President Lee's statements on Japan's lack of remorse for its colonization of the Korean Peninsula. The change of leadership in Seoul only deepened the rift as President Park continues to advocate to others the need for Japan to reflect on its past and take a more ''correct understanding of history.'' Pressures within South Korea, largely led by court cases appealing for greater South Korean Government activism to gain new compensation for victims of Japanese oppression during World War II, continue to make this a contentious issue, and sentiment in Japan toward South Korea has worsened considerably. The 50th anniversary of the bilateral peace treaty between Japan and South Korea next year will focus attention on this sensitive issue of remorse and compensation for WWII.

Finally, the rise of China is deepening the difficulties in the Japan-South Korea relationship. President Park began her time in office by visiting Washington and Beijing, but ignoring South Korea's longstanding diplomatic ties to Tokyo. Moreover, in high-level meetings with China, South Korean officials join with China to chastise Japan on its past history, creating the impression that Seoul and Beijing seek to isolate Japan diplomatically. While the historical legacy of World War II has long been a source of pain and friction in the diplomatic relations between Japan and South Korea, the growing synchronization of territorial disputes and criticism of Japanese leaders' positions on history between Seoul and Beijing make it difficult for Tokyo to manage. Popular sentiments in Tokyo have become very sensitive to this notion that Japan is the target of attack by its neighbors, just as popular sentiments in Seoul have become very sensitive to Japanese revisionist statements on the conflicts of the 20th century.

The U.S. role in these tensions is a difficult one. While U.S. interests are not served by the continuing estrangement between our two closest allies in Asia, Washington cannot broker a deal on the complex issue of historical memory. For reconciliation to occur, it must be undertaken directly by Tokyo and Seoul. Nonetheless, the United States must continue to urge President Park and Prime Minister Abe to take steps toward a concrete discussion on reconciliation, and to outline to both leaders the costs of their continued contention. Without leadership by both Park and Abe, this dispute could become much more difficult to resolve, and could undermine their ability to manage their own country's security. A comprehensive review of the path to restoring strong political and economic ties must be undertaken, and no preconditions to dialogue should be set.

The lost opportunities of this continued friction are real for the United States, and for the region. Close trilateral cooperation on North Korea is vital in case of a crisis or even worse, a conflict. U.S. access to bases in Japan is imperative to our ability to defend South Korea. Korean cooperation with Japan will be vital to ensuring the safety of Japanese citizens on the peninsula and in deterring North Korean aggression against Japan. Likewise, maritime cooperation between Seoul and Tokyo is essential for nonproliferation activities, as well as broader stability of East China Sea. Japan and Korea have a long history of coast guard and air defense cooperation, and should see this as an added stabilizer for the East China Sea, especially after the ADIZ. Furthermore, the ability of Tokyo and Seoul to cooperate in and around the East China Sea should become the basis for encouraging Chinese participation in similar risk reduction mechanisms, perhaps through the trilateral China, Japan, South Korea summitry. Finally, the frictions over their postwar settlement ultimately do affect the United States. More and more, U.S. citizens are raising questions about the historical disputes between Japan and South Korea, including the issue of compensation for the system of sexual slavery during WWII, and wondering about the rising nationalist impulses of both countries. There is plenty of room for nongovernmental discussions between U.S. and regional historians on some of these issues, and for U.S. engagement in a broader Asian discussion of historical memory. Our own leadership in demonstrating the importance of historical reconciliation has been a source of strengthening our relations with both countries. In both Korea and Japan, we must continue to emphasize the importance of reconciliation.

WHAT MORE CAN BE DONE?

President Obama's visit to both countries in April offers an opportunity to highlight the strengths not only of our bilateral ties, but also of the value of our trilateral partnership for regional security and prosperity. Elected representatives in Congress, too, should take every opportunity to demonstrate the importance of these alliances to the United States. Personal ties with the leaders of Japan and South Korea will allow for a more intimate dialogue on issues of reconciliation, and will allow for greater understanding of the changing security and economic concerns in the region. The United States has a tremendous stake in Asia, and our partnerships with both of these vibrant democracies and dynamic economies are indispensable to our own success. With Seoul and Tokyo, we have shared interests in a broad agenda of cooperation across the Asia-Pacific: freedom of navigation, the rule of law, an open and fair international economy, and the right of self-determination and territorial integrity. Finally, we must continue to invest in the next generation of alliance leaders, and the United States must continue to lean forward in funding, educating, and sending abroad our very best young minds. Building the personal relationships, and learning first hand about these two accomplished cultures, is one of the best means of ensuring the health of our relationships with Japan and South Korea in the generations ahead.

Senator CARDIN. Thank you, Dr. Smith.
Dr. Auslin.

STATEMENT OF MICHAEL AUSLIN, RESIDENT SCHOLAR, DIRECTOR OF JAPAN STUDIES, AMERICAN ENTERPRISE INSTITUTE, WASHINGTON, DC

Dr. AUSLIN. Mr. Chairman, thank you for the opportunity to come talk to you today about the status and trajectories of our alliances in Northeast Asia.

This hearing is being held at a particularly important time, for, as the United States continues a broad drawdown in military forces, the security trendline in Asia is worsening, not improving. Security in Asia remains based on our alliances which, for the past half century, have been focused on a handful of key nations, Japan and South Korea preeminent among them. As the committee understands, strengthening these alliances is one of the surest ways to maintain stability in the Asia-Pacific region, preserve U.S. influence, and help promote a future of greater freedom and prosperity for half our world.

You asked about the current status of the bilateral alliances and their progress. Regarding Japan, I would argue that we are witnessing a divergence between the politics and the policy of the United States-Japan alliance. While Washington applauds many of Prime Minister Shinzo Abe's measures to strengthen Japan's security and fulfill longstanding agreements with the United States, there is growing tension over perceptions of his approach to historical issues, such as the December visit to the controversial Yasukuni Shrine. While I argue that fears of the dangers of Mr. Abe's nationalism are overblown, we should be worried about the potential political divergence between Washington and Tokyo over the coming year.

As has been noted, South Korea and Washington continue to have close ties. In January 2014, we came to a new 5-year special measures agreement, under which Seoul will raise host-nation support payments for U.S. forces. However, one continuing source of uncertainty, which you have already highlighted, in this alliance is the so-called OPCON Transfer of Wartime Command of United States and South Korean Forces, which has already been delayed twice, and is most likely to be delayed after 2015.

The challenges we face this year, I think are threefold. The first, we have discussed several times here, is poor Japan-ROK relations. America's two closest allies barely speak to each other, and the tensions are at their highest in decades. While I have not been privy to what we have done to try to ameliorate that, Washington, I believe, should be doing much more behind closed doors in a very frank way to try and bridge the gap and stress common interests between our two allies.

The second challenge, also discussed here earlier, is North Korea, which, under Kim Jong-un, has become even more of a wildcard than before. I believe the administration does not appear to have any current initiatives to deal with the Kim regime. And, as long as there is a stalemate between North Korea and the rest of the world, Pyongyang wins.

In China, President Xi Jinping's first year in power saw new and destabilizing acts, such as the establishment of the East China Sea Air Defense Identification Zone. Having consolidated his power in his first year, he now has 9 full years to push forward, not only his program for domestic economic reform, which we should welcome, but also his national security objectives, which increasingly seem to be at odds with a stable Asia-Pacific region and dismissive of the Obama administration's rebalance.

There are areas for bilateral and trilateral cooperation in the coming year. Bilaterally with Japan, I agree with Dr. Smith that Washington must focus on preserving stability around the disputed Senkaku Islands. A greater American presence in the waters around the islands can help prevent an accident that causes conflict.

The economic basis of the United States-Japan relationship surely can be strengthened by concluding the Trans-Pacific Partnership talks, but we must recognize there remains a significant gulf between Washington and Tokyo, and the apparent death of fast-track trade promotion authority in the Senate means that any TPP agreement would find it difficult to get ratified.

With Seoul, we should be working on setting a realistic timeline for OPCON transfer, and also thinking of new initiatives for dealing with North Korea, such as stronger financial measures aimed at the Kim regime.

Many of these initiatives can be done in a trilateral fashion, such as greater cooperation and consultation on the ADIZ, on North Korea, and on building up missile defense. An innovative approach would be to try and expand the limited trilateral military exercises, which we currently conduct, or exploring limited joint training. Another idea is to consider a trilateral vision statement on the region's opportunities and challenges.

The Obama administration's rebalance has helped the American Government and public begin thinking about our interests in the post-Iraq and -Afghanistan world. Yet, the administration has also undercut its own policy, in two ways: firstly, through defense cuts that make it more difficult to maintain our presence abroad and call into question our long-term credibility, and secondly, by a hesitant approach to China's latest provocations that raise questions about our will to oppose their destabilizing actions. Washington must assure its friends and partners that it will not let the balance of power in Asia shift in favor of those who seek to use might to achieve their objectives. An Asia in which coercion is regularly employed cannot be an Asia that remains peaceful and prosperous in the long run.

In conclusion, there are three things that the administration, I think, should focus on. First is to clarify what its actual goals are in Asia, and make those goals clear to our allies and to those with whom we must deal. Second, Congress and the administration must ensure that our projected defense cuts do not further erode our readiness or our presence in Asia. And third, I argue, it is time for a new interagency strategic vision statement on Asia that lays out our interests and strategy. The result of such an approach would be stronger, liberal alliances and, quite likely, a region that is more stable and prosperous.

Thank you and I look forward to your questions.

[The prepared statement of Dr. Auslin follows:]

PREPARED STATEMENT OF DR. MICHAEL R. AUSLIN

Mr. Chairman, Ranking Member Rubio, members of the committee, thank you for the opportunity to come talk to you today about the status and trajectories of our alliances in Northeast Asia. This hearing is being held at a particularly important time, as the United States enters the final phase of winding down its combat role in Afghanistan and as the U.S. public begins looking forward to a future less focused on the Middle East. At the same time, several years of uncertainty regarding the U.S. defense budget are now being replaced by a better understanding of how our military will resize and reshape itself for the coming decade.

That said, the choices we are making as to our future foreign and security policies obviously do not take place in a vacuum. Other countries have their say as to how the world will look, and in part the future judgment on the wisdom of our likely course will be based on how other countries react to our policies. Nowhere is this more true than in Asia, where the world continues to watch, with equal parts envy and apprehension, the rise of China.

China continues to present a unique policy challenge to the United States. Our economic interdependence all but mandates close and smooth working relations at the public and private level; yet our political and security competition seems to grow without pause. This is the same dynamic faced by many of our allies and friends in Asia, to whom of course, the Janus-faced aspect of today's China is of enduring concern.

While the United States has broad-based economic, diplomatic, cultural, and social relationships with the nations of Asia, this hearing rightly seeks to understand the strengths and weaknesses of our alliance structure in Northeast Asia. Our alliances have been based for the past half-century on significant security commitments to a handful of key nations, Japan and South Korea preeminent among them. Because of this, China's activities in the region, as well as the ongoing North Korean nuclear and missile challenge, are the major influences on our alliance relations with Tokyo and Seoul.

Before discussing these two separately, it is important to note that our allies and partners in Asia are well aware of, and concerned about, projected drawdowns in the U.S. military. They are keenly attuned to how far the continental United States is from the flashpoints of Asia, such as the Korean Peninsula or the South China Sea. They read the headlines about our Navy shrinking to its smallest size since World War I and that the Air Force will shed hundreds of planes over the coming years. They find it hard to square such hard numbers with the constant statements of the Obama administration that it is rebalancing to the Asia-Pacific region. They worry that assurances by the United States Government that budget cuts at home will not affect the U.S. presence in Asia are mere rhetoric.

Indeed, both governments and publics in Asia are aware that U.S. military activity throughout the region is declining. Last year, Admiral Samuel Locklear, Commander of U.S. Pacific Command, testified before Congress that his travel budget had been cut by half. Similarly, the Pentagon has been forced to reduce military-to-military exchanges, such as postponing the Pacific Air Chiefs Symposium or canceling exercises run by Pacific Air Forces. General Hawk Carlisle, Commander of Pacific Air Forces, has been just one of the senior military leaders publicly to state his concern that resources have not followed the commitment to rebalance.

By raising expectations throughout the region that the United States would be more involved in Asian issues, we have created a dangerous gap with our inaction. While Secretary of State Kerry focused on climate change during his visit to China, South Korea, and Indonesia just 2 weeks ago, many of the nations of the region are far more concerned about the growing risk of conflict and what must be considered coercive behavior by China. Just last week, our ally the Philippines protested the Chinese use of water cannons by patrol boats on Philippine fishermen around the disputed Scarborough Shoal in the South China Sea. Asia's civilian airliners, except for Japan, are all complying with Beijing's intrusive demands for identification of peaceful flights over the East China Sea through China's new and unprecedented air defense identification zone (ADIZ). Japan continues to respond to regular incursions by Chinese vessels into the waters around the Senkaku Islands.

The nations of Asia watch very carefully Washington's hesitation and desire to avoid confronting China. They get clear messages from our actions that they must expect to deal with China on their own. They already perceive a shift in the balance of power, and we must recognize that at some point we will be seen as a paper tiger, whose commitments are not backed up by commensurate national will. Meanwhile, the trendline in Asia is worsening, not improving, making our lack of response all the more noticeable.

That said, our country retains a significant amount of influence in the Asia-Pacific region. This is due in no small part to the 325,000 men and women of U.S. Pacific Command, many of whom are forward deployed or on regular visits throughout the region. Our half-century old alliance structure also provides us with unique working relationships and the opportunity to remain involved with a core group of countries which themselves play diverse roles in Asia. As this committee understand, strengthening these alliances is one of the surest ways to help maintain stability in the Asia-Pacific region, preserve U.S. influence, and help promote a future of greater freedom and prosperity for half our world.

CURRENT STATUS OF BILATERAL ALLIANCES AND PROGRESS IN RECENT YEARS

Today, our bilateral alliances reflect the changes rippling through Asia as well as constraints here in the United States. To begin with Japan, I would argue that we are witnessing a divergence between the "politics" and the "policy" of the U.S.-Japan alliance. We are still in a delicate period that began in 2009, when the then-ruling Democratic Party of Japan (DPJ) upended the relationship by reopening the question of realigning U.S. forces in Japan. The core of the 2006 agreement that the DPJ decided to relitigate, so to speak, was the proposal to move Marine Corps Air Station Futenma out of its crowded urban location and relocate it to the less-populated northern part of Okinawa.

Fast-forward 5 years later and current Prime Minister Shinzo Abe, who resigned his position back in 2007, has moved to push the original agreement ahead and complete the Futenma Relocation Facility in Nago City. In addition, Mr. Abe has signaled his intention to reinterpret Japan's ban on exercising collective self-defense, which is something the United States has long wanted. He has confirmed his predecessor's decision to buy the F–35 Joint Strike Fighter and to loosen Japan's restrictions on arms exports. Much of this is codified in Tokyo's first-ever national security strategy. Just as significantly, Washington and Tokyo have agreed to revise the 1997 Mutual Defense Guidelines by the end of 2014 to update the alliance for the 21st century, including such new areas as the military use of space and cyber space. From this perspective, the policy of the U.S.-Japan alliance is moving in the right direction to respond to the new challenges it faces.

Yet, if the bilateral relationship is looked at from a "politics" perspective, Tokyo and Washington have moved from disagreement over policy to political tensions over perceptions of Prime Minister Abe's approach to historical issues. His December visit to the controversial Yasukuni Shrine resulted in a rare public reproach from the U.S. Embassy in Tokyo and strong condemnations by Beijing and Seoul. Statements by his appointees to Japan's public broadcaster have been criticized for their attempts to reinterpret Japan's wartime past. Fears that Prime Minister Abe is thinking of backing away from previous governments' statements on war-era comfort women have raised the ire of groups both in Asia and abroad. While I would argue that the fears of Mr. Abe's nationalism are overblown, we should be worried about the potential political divergence between Washington and Tokyo over the coming year.

However, whereas Japan and the United States continue to have difficulties in their relationship, the ties between Washington and Seoul remain extremely close. President Obama crafted an unusually tight relationship with former South Korean President Lee Myung-bak, and has continued the trend with current President Park Guen-hye. Uncomfortably for Tokyo, Presidents Obama and Park share similar sentiments regarding Prime Minister Abe's perceived historical revisionism. In terms of the U.S.–ROK working relationship, in January 2014, the United States and South Korea came to a new 5-year Special Measures Agreement (SMA), under which Seoul will raise its host nation support payments for U.S. forces in Korea by nearly 6 percent, increasing spending to around $870 million per year.

One continuing source of uncertainty in the alliance is the so-called "operational control" (OPCON) transfer of wartime command of U.S. and South Korean forces. Originally scheduled for 2007, it has been delayed twice at the request of the South Koreans, and is now planned for 2015, though that date, too, is likely to be pushed back. While our combined command structure in South Korea has resulted in an extraordinarily close training and working relationship between the two militaries,

Seoul's inability to successfully develop the capabilities needed to lead military operations in wartime is a source of concern.

With both Seoul and Tokyo modernizing their militaries, Washington can look forward to a future with ever more capable allies. Both countries are likely to purchase the F–35 fighter and each has ballistic missile defense capabilities, such as modern Aegis-equipped guided missile cruisers. Each also has been the target of cyber attacks, and both are thus focused on increasing their cyber defense capabilities.

One major difficulty for the United States in Asia is the poor state of bilateral relations between Japan and South Korea. America's two closest allies barely speak to each other, and tensions are at their highest in decades. Part of this is due to the historical issue I noted above, but it also derives from the continuing dispute over the Takeshima/Dokdo Islands in the Sea of Japan (terminology over this body of water was settled by the State Department in 2012). The lack of trust and bitter feelings between the two countries makes it difficult to optimize the U.S. presence in Northeast Asia. Instead of having two allies working closely together, U.S. military planners must conduct most of their operations on two bilateral tracks. Given that the common threat from North Korea, and now antagonistic behavior from China, such as the ADIZ, affects both, Tokyo and Seoul would be well advised to put aside some of their differences and embrace their similarities. Sadly, there seems no prospect of this happening anytime in the near future.

Challenges for 2014

The challenges we face in our Northeast Asian bilateral alliances this year are threefold: first, the poor state of Japan-ROK relations; second, North Korea; and third, Chinese provocations. This list has been steady for quite some time, and is unlikely to change soon.

I have already briefly discussed the tensions in the Japan-ROK relationship, but it is worth mentioning here that, if anything, ties seem to be getting worse. Despite their deep economic links, and their shared liberal values such as rule law, freedom of the press, and the like, they find the tensions between them at historically high levels. President Park appears to desire to draw closer to China at Japan's expense, and has steadfastly refused to meet Prime Minister Abe. She has taken the opportunity of visits by senior American officials, such as Vice President Biden, to publicly criticize Japan. For their part, leading Japanese now openly talk about "Seoul fatigue," and a growing resentment against President Park's refusal to reciprocate to Japanese outreach. This is a serious state of affairs, and while the United States cannot make the two nations end their feud, Washington should be doing much more behind closed doors to make clear that our patience is not infinite, and that we cannot be as effective as we want to be if we cannot work in a trilateral fashion with our two most important allies in Asia.

The second major challenge this year is the unending crisis that is North Korea. It is disheartening to say that we currently know even less about what is happening inside Pyongyang than we did during the rule of the late Kim Jong-il. Since executing his uncle late last year, Kim Jong-un has become even more of a wildcard and enigma than his predecessors. By continuing his family's long-term pursuit of nuclear weapons and ballistic missile technology, he has dashed the hopes of some who saw in him an incipient reformer, partial to Disney characters. We no longer have confidence that China retains its traditional influence over the Kim family, as tenuous as that may have been, nor are we any better at anticipating Pyongyang's next provocative act.

The six-party talks, designed to solve the nuclear crisis, have been stalled since 2008, and the Obama administration's one attempt at a deal, the 2012 Leap Day Agreement, was broken by the Kim regime just months after its signing. The administration does not appear to have any current initiatives to deal with North Korea, and U.N. sanctions continue to be undercut by China. As long as there is a stalemate between North Korea and the rest of the world, Pyongyang wins. Even the devastating U.N. report detailing human rights abuses and the crimes against humanity that are regularly perpetrated by Pyongyang seems to have had little effect on galvanizing some type of approach to put more pressure on this heinous regime. Moreover, the longer America waits and watches developments in the country, the more competent North Korea becomes in its nuclear and missile programs.

Nor is there much reason to be confident about the trajectory of China. Unlike his immediate predecessors, President Xi Jinping has consolidated his power in his first year in office. He appears to have better control over the military than former President Hu Jintao ever did, and has streamlined his country's national security decisionmaking process. He now has 9 full years to push forward not only his program for domestic economic reform, which the United States should welcome, but also his national security objectives, which increasingly seem to be at odds with a stable Asia-Pacific region.

President Xi's first year saw new and destabilizing acts, such as the establishment of the East China Sea air defense identification zone. Provocations over the Senkakus also increased, with reports of Chinese fighter jets being sent near the area and an instance of a Chinese naval vessel locking its firing radar on a Japanese Maritime Self-Defense ship. If these are any indications to go by, President Xi is comfortable pushing the boundaries of provocative behavior. That is the reason the trendline in Asia is negative, and is not improving despite regular high-level U.S.-Chinese interaction, such as the Sunnylands summit between Presidents Obama and Xi last year and Vice President Biden's visit to Beijing last December.

It appears that the Chinese Government has calculated that it can continue its assertive, even coercive, actions in the face of America's protestations that it is rebalancing to the Pacific. Tensions are running high enough in Northeast Asia to cause Prime Minister Abe to remark at Davos earlier this year that Sino-Japanese relations are in a pre-1914 stage. As of now, it does not seem that Washington has come up with a successful policy that can encourage Beijing to act in a constructive manner on security issues, while continuing its integration into the world economy. Not surprisingly, many believe this is the greatest foreign policy challenge our country will face in the coming generation.

Areas for bilateral and trilateral cooperation in 2014

Given the challenges in Northeast Asia faced by us and by our allies Japan and South Korea, there are important areas of cooperation that Washington can explore. Bilaterally with Japan, Washington should work to clarify how it can help preserve stability around the disputed Senkaku islands, including in the air domain. While war between Japan and China over the Senkakus is a remote possibility, there is a much higher likelihood that an accident could cause a true crisis, and perhaps even limited conflict. Although the U.S. Government has chosen not to take a position on the sovereignty claims by Japan and China, it recognizes Japan's long-standing administration of the islands. Thus, showing support for Japan through a greater American presence in the immediate waters around the islands does not seem like a provocation on our part.

In addition, continuing expanded military exercises between U.S. and Japanese forces, such as last month's Iron Fist exercise in California with U.S. Marines and Japanese Ground Self-Defense Force units, will help the Japanese military become a more capable force and more credible in its new focus on protecting Japan's southwestern islands from threat. There is also room for more cooperation between the U.S. Air Force and Japan Air Self-Defense Force in refusing to recognize China's ADIZ over the East China Sea. Such activities have a clear diplomatic component, as well, and can serve to promote a clear vision of U.S. engagement in the region.

Finally, the economic basis of the U.S.-Japan relationship can be strengthened by a timely conclusion of the Trans-Pacific Partnership talks. Unfortunately, the recent round of negotiations in Singapore showed that there remains a significant gulf between Washington and Tokyo on import tariffs, especially for agricultural goods. On top of that, the apparent death of "fast track" Trade Promotion Authority in the Senate means that any TPP agreement would find it difficult to get ratified. There are also reports that foreign negotiators are hesitant to make any agreement if they cannot be assured of fast track status in the U.S. Senate. The Obama administration must push both at home and in Tokyo to better sell the benefits of a high-standards free trade agreement.

Washington's interest in North Korean denuclearization means that 2014 should be a year of new initiatives with Seoul. To let another 12 months go by without any new approach to pressuring North Korea means that Kim Jong-un will further strengthen himself. Recommitting to financial sanctions against the Kim family and its lieutenants may be one way of bringing them back to the table, but the State Department must work with Seoul and Tokyo to have a united front in the face of Chinese opposition. On the security side of the U.S.–ROK alliance, clarifying Seoul's readiness for OPCON transfer will help remove future uncertainty. Working, as well, to improve South Korea's ballistic missile defense capability can provide some assurance that threats from the North can be answered.

Most of these initiatives could be done in a trilateral fashion, since Japan and South Korea face similar security challenges. There is, however, little to no likelihood of Seoul and Tokyo agreeing to work more closely on their own. Nonetheless, the Obama administration should push firmly for more trilateral cooperation and consultation on the ADIZ, on North Korea, and on building up missile defense capabilities. Blunt talk about the costs of their diplomatic freeze may help move forward quiet initiatives, such as trilateral negotiations on North Korea.

An innovative approach would be to try and expand the limited trilateral military exercises that we current conduct. Exploring limited joint training is another way to help build trust between the two country's defense forces. Another idea is to consider a trilateral vision statement on the region's opportunities and challenges. Such a diplomatic document by the liberal leaders in Northeast Asia could even develop into a larger document bringing in such stalwart U.S. allies as Australia and those that feel increasing pressure from China, like the Philippines.

How to Create Stronger, Like-Minded Alliances?

In making the rebalance a central part of its foreign policy strategy, the Obama administration has helped the American Government and public begin thinking about our interests in the post-Iraq and Afghanistan world. Recognizing the dynamic nature of the Asia-Pacific, its crucial importance to the global economy, its opportunity to help promote democracy, but also its security challenges is the beginning of setting American foreign and security policy on a new path.

Yet the administration has also undercut its own policy in two ways: firstly, through defense cuts that make it more difficult to maintain U.S. presence abroad and call into question our long-term credibility; and secondly, by a hesitant approach to China's latest provocations that raise questions about our will in opposing destabilizing actions.

Our allies, foremost among them Japan, have raised concerns about the competing priorities of the Obama administration. They worry that the rebalance is empty rhetoric and that Washington is all too eager to avoid antagonizing China. Both Seoul and Tokyo wonder if Washington is doing everything it can to blunt North Korea's plans to become a full nuclear power. They are concerned that we are too laissez faire about the balance of power, or perceptions of the balance of power, in Asia.

It is in American interests to make clear to our allies that it is their responsibility to protect their own territory. But Washington must also assure its friends and partners that it will not let the balance of power in Asia shift in favor of those who seek to use might to achieve their objectives. An Asia in which coercion is regularly employed cannot be an Asia that remains peaceful and prosperous in the long run.

There is much that we can do to ensure our resolve is clearly understood. The most important step the administration can take is to clarify for itself what its actual goals are in Asia. This was perhaps one of the key failings of the rebalance: it never articulated what the administration desired to accomplish. Is it to blunt China's assertive behavior, to promote democracy and liberalism, or to open markets? For example, the administration never fully explained why it was seeking more rotational basing opportunities for U.S. forces in Asia, which was perhaps the most visible of its rebalancing moves.

The nations of Asia well understand that Washington and Beijing have very different visions for Asia's future. The administration would do well to recognize the reality that we and the Chinese unfortunately agree on very little and have competing goals. We can and should continue to try and work with the Chinese, but the clearest signal would be sent to our Northeast and Southeast Asian allies if we appeared to understand what is evident to everyone in the region: China seeks to build its power and influence to a point where it has the freedom of action to carry out any policy that it desires. While there is little reason to believe Beijing wants war or any type of conflict, it appears increasingly willing to risk hostilities because it believes that no one will oppose it.

Second, Congress and the administration must do everything possible to ensure that current and projected defense cuts do not further erode our readiness or our presence in Asia. If the numbers of planes and ships in Asia start to dip, it will be harder to maintain our credibility. Joint exercises and military exchanges need to be fully funded, so that partner militaries believe that we remain a steadfast friend to them.

Third, strategic planning exercises, like the Quadrennial Defense Review, should not be budget-driven documents, but rather explore what the military really needs in order to maintain its qualitative superiority in Asia. What types of weapons systems are best suited to Asia's unique challenges of distance and potential adversaries with growing capabilities? How can we take advantage of asymmetric means of defense? Once we have done that, then the Pentagon needs to reach out to Tokyo and Seoul to discuss the best ways in which they can build to their strengths and complement our investments.

In short, in order to build like-minded alliances, both Congress and the pubic should push the administration to be clear-eyed about the challenges we face, openly discuss them, and have a realistic plan for meeting them. That would reassure our allies that we truly put our shared values at the center of our foreign policy and that we will not ignore the actions of those who seek to destabilize Asia in their favor. The result of such an approach will be stronger liberal alliances and quite likely a region that is more stable and prosperous.

Senator CARDIN. Well, thank you both. You have given a good overview of the strengths and what we have been able to accomplish in the rebalance, but also the challenges that lie ahead.

And I was listening to both of your testimonies. I was struck by the maritime security issues that we talk about a great deal. Rather explosive. We are worried that it could trigger a major incident at any time. And thinking about the events over the past week in Ukraine, where Russia, for the second time, is using its military force to take control over lands that do not belong to Russia. There is no dispute that Crimea is Ukrainian territory, yet Russia is using its military there. And in the China Seas, the dominant military force is probably China. And we are all concerned as to whether they are going to just use military might, causing an incident. And now, if Russia's activities in Ukraine go unchallenged, does this raise the concern that China could use that as an example for its own military actions in disputed areas?

Either one of you.

Dr. SMITH. Thank you, Mr. Chairman. I will start off the answer to that very complex question.

I think last year I took a fairly careful look at the maritime risks inherent in China's new contestation of the Senkaku issues. And so, I would like to submit that for the record here, the——

Senator CARDIN. Absolutely. It will be made part of our record.

Dr. SMITH [continuing]. Council on Foreign Relations report on that. The United States has very deep interests, obviously, in any kind of incident, be it very small or in gray-zone areas or a more direct military confrontation in the East China Sea, so we have to be very careful in our thinking, but also talk very closely with Japan about its thinking about how it might manage a response to the Chinese.

[EDITOR'S NOTE.—The Council on Foreign Relations report mentioned above can be found in the "Additional Material Submitted for the Record" section at the end of this hearing.]

Dr. SMITH. I do not know that I would be ready quite yet to extrapolate from the Ukrainian situation into Chinese behavior. I have watched, over the last couple of days, China's initial responses to this, and they seem, themselves, quite cautious yet. I think there is an opportunity to engage with China, through the U.N. and directly, on its understanding of the situation in the Ukraine, and I think we ought to, with a particular emphasis on Chinese practices, as well.

But, I think the escalatory path that I imagine in the East China Sea is one that could be direct, could come out of the island dispute, but could also be an opportunity that presents itself in a different confrontation; for example, a conflict on the Korean Peninsula, or, as you say, perhaps even elsewhere around the globe.

I think the Japanese are particularly concerned about their readiness and their ability to respond, should China move against these disputed islands. And our ability to help them in making sure that they are ready to respond effectively, I think, will be very, very important.

Senator CARDIN. Thank you.

Dr. Auslin.

Dr. AUSLIN. Mr. Chairman, thank you for raising that.

I think the short answer is, yes. And I think it is probably equally useful to look in the other direction, which is to say, What has Vladimir Putin seen in our reactions, or lack of reactions, to what China has been doing in this region for several years?—to say whether that may have encouraged his assessment of our willingness to—and the West's willingness, overall—to opposed his recent moves.

I agree, I think that China is misjudging Japan's willingness to defend the Senkakus for as long as is entirely possible. And we just recently saw a move, out of the Japanese, to set up a new quick-response force of 3,000 forces that would be designed specifically for amphibious combat and to respond to any threats to the islands.

But, in terms of what China, itself, is taking away from the Ukraine situation, the Chinese Foreign Ministry has come out with a statement supporting what Russia is doing. So, it is clear on which side they are aligning themselves. There is a consistency, in terms of their willingness to support destabilizing actors and actions around the world, and this is no different.

Whether or not this, as Dr. Smith said, extrapolates into their willingness to raise the risk level and use force regarding the Senkakus, I would just simply say, I think the trendline has already moved in that direction. We and the Japanese have made very clear the ways in which we want this to be resolved peacefully. And yet, now we have an ADIZ, we have broader claims over the waters, and the spread of this to away from just patrol boats to the navy itself. So, I think we should be worried about the risk line, and certainly the lessons that Beijing is getting from watching our responses to other such provocations around the world.

Thank you.

Senator CARDIN. Well, I thank you for that observation. It does have us very concerned. Another reason why how Ukraine is ultimately resolved is so important.

Both of you have raised the dilemma of our relationship with Japan and the Republic of Korea and, so far, our inability to strengthen the ties between those two countries. So, what would you suggest that we could do that could get two allies that have strong views about each other to look to the future rather than to the past, recognizing the responsibility to acknowledge the historical issues?

Dr. AUSLIN. Well, Mr. Chairman, if there were an easy solution to that answer, you know, we would all be celebrating it, and I am sure it would have been implemented. I think, again, what we need to be concerned about, at one level, is the trendline. And the trendline is, these relations are getting worse, they are not getting better. Whether China, itself, is seeking to put a wedge between South Korea and Japan, clearly President Park of South Korea has seen it in her own interest to move closer to China, to move away from what had been a fairly good working relationship with Japan. And that is something that has not improved over the year. And, in fact, Mr. Chairman, I would argue that that was probably a lot of the decision, going into the decision that Prime Minister Abe made to visit the shrine in December, quite frankly. You noted that it came on the first anniversary of his coming back into office. And I think he gave a year to try to see how these relations were going to work with both China and South Korea, and, at the end of it, concluded that he had very little to lose by doing what he thought was right for his own domestic constituency, and send a message that is—Japan would be looking out for its own interests.

Again, I do not know what is going on behind closed doors, but I think there comes a time where we, given our commitments to both of these countries, need to be extraordinarily blunt and have a real heart-to-heart talk, so to speak, with both of them about the problems this is causing. And I would argue, quite frankly, that our patience is not infinite; that, to the degree that this makes our job harder for them, then they need to not only think about what that might ultimately cause, in terms of the ability of the United States to fulfill its commitments, but also how we may rethink what is in our own best interests.

Thank you.

Dr. SMITH. Thank you, Mr. Chairman.

I think the President's visit—President Obama's visit to the two capitals in April provides an opportunity, at the highest level, for the President to convey his concerns to both Prime Minister Abe and to President Park. I do think that there was a certain movement that we could see going on, on the part of governments in South Korea and Japan, toward the end of last year. Very initial discussions with our team here in Washington and people in the think-tank world, as well, to sort of feel our way through of what a comprehensive discussion might look like between these two countries. Unfortunately, Prime Minister Abe's visit to Yasukuni, I think, has set that back somewhat.

I do think reconciliation, the final reconciliation between these two countries, needs to incorporate a broad host of issues. South Koreans are very concerned about Mr. Abe's views on history, have asked him, directly and repeatedly, to reaffirm his commitment to both the Murayama and the Kono statements. I think, on the side of the Japanese, I hear often that reopening the basis of the 1965 treaty, restarting again a conversation about compensation and settlements, when that was diplomatically accounted for in 1965, that would be a problem on the Japanese side. So, I think you have bookends at both ends here within which the Japanese and South Korean leaders will have to discuss what they think is possible.

I do think that the power of the Presidency is great, and the President's direct engagement with these two leaders may provide some stimulus to a conversation, perhaps a trilateral meeting later this year at the UNGA meeting in September, for example, may be another opportunity, down the road.

Thank you.

Senator CARDIN. I would strongly support what you are saying about the President's visit, and I would hope he would have concrete suggestions, not just, ''You need to improve the relationship,'' but steps that could be taken by both leaders in doing that.

I had a chance to meet with both leaders in May in their respective capitals, and I sensed a real interest in trying to move forward. But, since that time, just the reverse has taken place.

One final question or observation for you, and that is, in Japan, the interpretation of their constitution to allow for self-defense I think makes it possible that Japan will take its military presence to a new level. Is that a positive or a negative or just a reality type of observation? Is this something that we should be concerned about, or is this a natural evolution for Japan?

Dr. SMITH. Thank you, Mr. Chairman, for that question.

I think the interpretation of collective self-defense has been outlined by the Abe Cabinet in a very specific way. And I suspect that, in April, the report of his advisory committee will be issued, and we will see the government develop very concretely what it means when it says that the Japanese military should be able to work alongside the United States military and perhaps other countries in the region in humanitarian and disaster capacities. So, I think we will get more granularity to the concept that the Abe government is putting forward in the next 5 to 6 months.

I also suspect that the United States Department of Defense and the Japanese Ministry of Defense will be talking very carefully about how this will affect and enhance alliance cooperation on a number of the kinds of contingencies that we have talked about here this afternoon.

I am not so much worried about the progress of this discussion, in large part because I trust the democratic practices of Japan. Their legislature will be very involved in that discussion, and I do not think you are going to see any government, be it Mr. Abe's or any others, be able to move the Japanese people in a direction that they do not want to go.

So, I suspect you will have a very full parliamentary discussion this coming fall and that you will hear all kinds of viewpoints representing the popular sentiments and concerns inside Japan about reinterpreting that particular piece of Japan's Constitution.

Thank you.

Dr. AUSLIN. Mr. Chairman, I would just say, we should be concerned only if it does not go through. I think that it is an extraordinarily important step for Japan that is part of moves that have been undertaken by both the Democratic Party, when it was in power, and now under Mr. Abe, which is, for example, buying the F–35s and the increase in their abilities in ballistic missile defense, as we have seen.

Allowing for a reinterpretation of the right to the exercise of collective self-defense will only help Japan become an exporter of security, and that is something we want to see. We want to see Japan not be as isolated as it has been for many of its neighbors, but to—as much as it has done work on things like counterterrorism and antiterrorism, on—its Coast Guard is active around the region. This is an extraordinary opportunity for Japan to become truly engaged with its neighbors in a way that removes ambiguity about its commitment to stability in the region. And so, anything that we can do to encourage this or encourage the process within the structures of the alliance, I think we should be doing.

Thank you.

Senator CARDIN. Well, once again, thank both of you for your very helpful testimony before the subcommittee. And I will look forward to reading the report that you have submitted for our review.

We are going to keep the committee record open until close of business Friday, in the likelihood that members may have questions that they would like to submit for the record. If you are the recipient of those questions, we ask that you try to respond as promptly as possible.

And, with that, the subcommittee will stand adjourned.

Thank you.

[Whereupon, at 4:05 p.m., the hearing was adjourned.]

ADDITIONAL MATERIAL SUBMITTED FOR THE RECORD

RESPONSE OF DAVID F. HELVEY TO QUESTION SUBMITTED BY SENATOR BENJAMIN L. CARDIN

FUTENMA REPLACEMENT FACILITY

Question. The relocation of Marine Corps Air Station Futenma in Okinawa has been a thorn in the side of the alliance for over 15 years, although the Okinawan Governor's landfill permit approval late last year was an important milestone that should allow for more progress with this project. You stated that the realignment and movement of troops to Guam is "on-track."

♦ Is the Department of Defense confident that Japan and the United States are on the same page when it comes to the sequencing and funding for the Futenma Replacement Facility and the movement of troops to Guam?

♦ Are the stakeholders in this process prepared to make timely decisions and take care of their own responsibilities efficiently?

Answer. The Department has closely coordinated with the Government of Japan to ensure that we have a common plan for sequencing and funding of the realignment initiatives on Okinawa and Guam, including the Futenma Replacement Facility. This multifaceted effort is regularly reviewed to take into account both actual and anticipated changes occurring in the implementation of this plan.

As part of this review process, working together with our GoJ counterparts, and taking into account variables such as available funding, construction capacity and sequencing, and collateral construction requirements, we have and will continue to make adjustments to the plan in as efficient and timely a manner as possible.

COUNCIL *on*
FOREIGN
RELATIONS

Center for Preventive Action

CONTINGENCY PLANNING MEMORANDUM NO. 18

A Sino-Japanese Clash in the East China Sea

Sheila A. Smith
April 2013

Author Bio

Sheila A. Smith is senior fellow for Japan studies at the Council on Foreign Relations.

A Sino-Japanese Clash in the East China Sea

INTRODUCTION

Tensions have risen to dangerous levels between Japan and China over a small group of uninhabited islands in the East China Sea, called the Senkaku by the Japanese and the Diaoyu by the Chinese. These islands were once controlled by the United States as part of its post–World War II occupation of Japan and only returned to Japanese administrative control with the reversion of Okinawa in 1971. As Washington prepared to return these islands to Japan, the People's Republic of China (PRC) and Taiwan contested Japan's sovereignty. Two years earlier, a United Nations (UN) geological survey of the East China Sea revealed the potential of significant hydrocarbon resources. Contending sovereignty claims over the islands thus have both historical and resource-related dimensions.

Until recently, this territorial dispute was little more than a minor irritant in Sino-Japanese relations. However, against the backdrop of China's growing military power, the island dispute has increased concerns in Tokyo about Beijing's regional intentions and the adequacy of Japan's security, while stoking nationalistic politics in both capitals. Political miscalculation in Tokyo or Beijing, or unintended military interactions in and around the disputed islands, could escalate further, leading to an armed clash between Asia's two largest powers. The United States, as a treaty ally of Japan but with vital strategic interests in fostering peaceful relations with China, has a major stake in averting such a clash and resolving the dispute, if possible.

THE CONTINGENCIES

Sino-Japanese tensions in the East China Sea have been building steadily since 2010, when a Chinese fishing trawler rammed two Japan Coast Guard (JCG) vessels in waters near the Senkaku/Diaoyu Islands and Japan detained the captain. Although the crisis was eventually defused, the territorial dispute came to a head again in September 2012, when Japanese prime minister Yoshihiko Noda announced his government's decision to purchase three of the five islands. The islands were privately owned, but a new wave of activism, including Chinese attempts to land on the islands and a public campaign by the Tokyo governor to purchase them himself, prompted Noda to attempt to neutralize nationalist pressures. The decision triggered widespread anti-Japanese demonstrations in China, resulting in extensive damage to Japanese companies operating there. Eventually China dampened the popular response, but it has since repeatedly stated its intent to assert its own administrative control over the disputed islands. China's Marine Surveillance agency intensified its patrols of the waters in and around the islands, and China's Bureau of Fisheries patrols followed suit. The JCG in turn increased its patrols and put them on 24/7 alert.

The danger of escalation to armed conflict increased when the two militaries became directly involved. On December 13, 2012, a small Chinese reconnaissance aircraft entered undetected into Japanese airspace above the islands. The JCG alerted Japan's Air Self-Defense Force (ASDF), which scrambled fighter jets based in Naha, Okinawa; however, they were too late to intercept. In January, China sent its reconnaissance aircraft back toward the islands accompanied by fighter jets, but stopped short of entering Japan's airspace, and no direct aerial confrontation occurred. Japan's Maritime Self-Defense Force (MSDF) reported that a Chinese frigate locked its firing radar on the Japanese destroyer *Yudachi* on January 30, 2013. Chinese authorities instigated an investigation into the incident in response to Japan's protest, leading to speculation that Beijing was unaware of the ship captain's actions. Although China's Ministry of Defense later denied that the incident took place, it did acknowledge the danger such an act posed.

Given current circumstances in the East China Sea, three contingencies are conceivable: first, an accidental or unintended incident in and around the disputed islands could trigger a military escalation of the crisis; second, either country could make a serious political miscalculation in an effort to demonstrate sovereign control; and third, either country could attempt to forcibly control the islands.

Accidental/Unintended Military Incident

Although recent incidents have sensitized China and Japan to the risk of accidental and unintended military interactions, the danger will persist while emotions run high and their forces operate in close proximity. In stressful and ambiguous times, when decision-making is compressed by the speed of modern weapons systems, the risk of human error is higher. The 2001 collision between a U.S. reconnaissance aircraft and a Chinese fighter jet near Hainan Island is a case in point, as was the intrusion of a Chinese Han submarine in Japanese territorial waters in 2004. So-called rules of engagement (ROEs), intended to guide and control the behavior of local actors, are typically general in scope and leave room for personal interpretation that may lead to actions that escalate a crisis situation. Compounding the risk of unintended escalation between Chinese and Japanese air and naval units is the unpredictable involvement of third parties such as fishermen or civilian activists who may attempt to land on the islands. Their actions could precipitate an armed response by either side.

Political Miscalculation in an Effort to Demonstrate Sovereign Control

Political miscalculation of either country's intent or resolve, as well as miscalculation of the U.S. position, could lead to armed conflict. First, Japan and China are already finding it difficult to read each other's actions. Past Japanese government leasing of the Senkaku/Diaoyu Islands effectively kept nationalist activists—Japanese as well as Chinese and Taiwanese—at bay. In mid-2012, however, rising nationalist sentiments during leadership transitions inflamed the dispute. This stimulated heated debate in Tokyo over how to consolidate Japanese sovereignty and was a factor in the December 2012 election of conservative prime minister Shinzo Abe, who advocated inhabiting the islands. This escalation in asserting sovereignty claims through the use of patrols, populating the islands, and perhaps even military defense of the territory could lead to heightened tensions between the two countries and whip up nationalist sentiments, potentially limiting the capacity of leaders to peacefully manage the dispute.

Second, China could miscalculate U.S. interests and intentions. Since last year, U.S. policymakers have sought to lessen tensions but have also taken steps to clarify the U.S. role in deterring any coercive action by China. U.S. and Japanese forces have conducted regular exercises to strengthen defense of Japan's southwestern islands and maritime surveillance capabilities. Both former secretary of state Hillary Clinton and former secretary of defense Leon Panetta clearly stated that the United States will defend Japan against any aggression, and on November 29, 2012, the U.S. Senate passed a resolution accompanying the 2013 National Defense Authorization Act to demonstrate congressional support for the Obama administration's commitment to Japan's defense. As tensions escalated late last year, Washington increased its deployments in and around Japan. Early this year, as military interactions raised the potential for conflict, Clinton restated the U.S. position that it would not accept any unilateral attempt to wrest control of the islands. Still, Beijing could miscalculate Washington's commitment to defend Japan and/or seek to test that commitment. Finally, U.S. assurances could lead Tokyo to overestimate Washington's response and to act in a manner that would increase the chance for confrontation. To date, however, Tokyo has tended to err on the side of caution in planning and exercises with U.S. forces, and it is unlikely Japan would act without evidence of U.S. assistance.

Deliberate Action to Forcibly Establish Control Over Islands

Although this seems highly unlikely today, either party could take military action to assert sovereignty over the disputed islands. Rising domestic pressures or an unexpected opportunity for a fait accompli could lead to a decision by either government to establish military control over the territory.

WARNING INDICATORS

Although it seems that neither Tokyo nor Beijing wants to use force to pursue its interests in the territorial dispute, it is possible that either government could choose to do so in the future. Indicators of a strategic decision by either country to escalate tensions include:

- *Introduction of Japanese or Chinese military forces on or in the vicinity of the islands to claim or defend sovereignty.* Japan and China have kept their militaries distant from the disputed islands; a military presence would intensify the dispute and raise the probability of armed conflict.
- *Deliberate use of economic sanctions.* China's informal embargo on rare-earth exports to Japan during the 2010 crisis and the setback to Japanese investment in the latter half of 2012 suggest a new role for economic instruments of pressure in this dispute. The imposition of sanctions (i.e., embargos, boycotts, or blockades) to harm economic performance would signal a desire to escalate conflict. Government action to reduce conspicuously economic dependence would be a lesser but equally important indicator of a strategic shift.
- *Government-sponsored nationalist activism.* Nationalist activism has until now come from a host of social actors, including fishermen, local politicians, and advocacy groups. A deliberate effort by either government to stimulate popular nationalism against the other nation would signal a shift in intentions away from resolving the territorial dispute peacefully. Government calls to mobilize popular support for the defense of the islands, lift regulatory controls over access to the islands, or elect leaders who advocate sustained confrontation over the sovereignty dispute would be indicators of a strategic shift in the conflict.

Short of a deliberate effort to exert physical control over the Senkaku/Diaoyu Islands, several specific indicators raise the likelihood of an inadvertent clash between Japan and China:

- *Incident involving the loss of life in the waters off the disputed islands.* No lives have been lost over the disputed islands, but should these interactions result in the loss of life, crisis management would be a serious challenge for both governments. China's Bureau of Fisheries and its Marine Surveillance patrols have increased the tempo of operations near the disputed islands. JCG ROEs give ship commanders the authority to respond; the ROEs for Chinese paramilitary agencies are less clear. In addition, fishing boats from Taiwan accompanied by their coast guard have periodically complicated the standoff.

- *A protracted airborne standoff between Japanese and Chinese forces in the East China Sea.* China's intrusion into Japan's airspace prompted Prime Minister Abe's cabinet to review its air defenses. Heightened Japanese sensitivity over the territorial dispute with China could raise the stakes for Japan's air force if Chinese forces test their readiness in the vicinity of the islands.

- *Loss of national command control over local commanders.* Local commanders could act independently in ways that are interpreted as presaging hostile intent (such as the Chinese radar lock on Japanese forces), which could trigger a defensive response that escalates the crisis. Local commanders will be hard-pressed to remain calm should interactions increase near the islands, especially if miscalculations continue. Postwar constitutional constraints on Japan's military have produced well-articulated principles and procedures for civilian control over the SDF, with clearly established ROEs and careful central government oversight over local forces. Civil-military command structures in China are less clear and not well described. Moreover, the degree of oversight of local commanders by Beijing is also unknown. Strong central government command over local forces will be absolutely essential to avoid unintended incidents from escalating.

IMPLICATIONS FOR U.S. INTERESTS

The United States has major interests at stake in the growing tension between Japan and China. Three risks in particular stand out:

- *Risk of armed hostilities with China.* U.S. forward-deployed forces are deeply integrated with Japan's SDF and assist with intelligence, surveillance, and reconnaissance (ISR) support, as well as exercises designed to enhance Japan's defense capabilities. U.S. forces may be asked to assist Japan's SDF in the case of a broader military conflict, and would likely provide logistical support as well as continued ISR collaboration. Direct armed conflict with China would harm a broad array of vital U.S. economic, political, and strategic interests.

- *Risk to U.S.-Japan alliance.* The U.S. response to a Japan-China conflict would determine the future of the U.S.-Japan alliance, as well as other alliances in the Asia Pacific. Tokyo remains concerned that Washington might not fulfill its treaty obligations if Beijing escalates the conflict, and U.S. government statements of its intentions notwithstanding, domestic perceptions in Japan of U.S. hesitancy in the case of Chinese coercion will shape Japan's future security choices. Japan's postwar policy of military self-restraint and reliance on the United States for strategic protection, including its continued abnegation of nuclear weapons, would likely come to an end if the United States chose not to defend Japan against Chinese aggression.

- *Risk to regional stability.* China's dispute with the Philippines over the Scarborough Reef in the South China Sea has set a particularly dangerous precedent. Many leaders in the Asia-Pacific region are beginning to see China's maritime behavior as unpredictable and will be watching to see if Washington ultimately resists or accommodates Chinese military pressure on its periphery. The Japanese case will be decisive not only for Japan's future choices but for many other allies and friends in the region adjusting to the rise of China.

PREVENTIVE OPTIONS

The United States has considerable interest in doing all that it can to prevent armed conflict between Japan and China. The policies for preventing such a conflict include the following steps.

Deter and Dissuade Unilateral Actions to Contest Japan's Administrative Control of the Islands

Washington can regularly and consistently communicate its interest in, and position on, the island dispute to avoid ambiguity in the U.S. security commitment to Japan. Privately, Washington could also communicate to both capitals the need to avoid statements and assertions that would incite popular sentiments on the dispute and encourage peaceful dispute resolution.

To deter potential Chinese assertiveness, the United States can consult closely with Japan on its response to Chinese activities near the disputed islands, and can ensure seamless U.S.-Japan defense cooperation. To counter any impulse toward Japanese assertiveness, Washington and Tokyo should confirm the conditions under which U.S. defense assistance would be rendered. Japan's leaders remain committed to limiting their use of military force to defensive missions. Should that change, U.S. policymakers should revisit the terms of defense assistance.

U.S. forces can also assist Japanese agencies in a maritime emergency, should an incident involving the Japanese and Chinese militaries occur. For example, Washington can urge Tokyo to update communications and exercises between the JCG and MSDF, providing assistance if needed. To date, there has been little need for Japan to integrate its civilian maritime policing with its defense operations. As Chinese maritime forces in the East China Sea expand and the distinction between civil and military maritime forces becomes less clear, Japan can develop its planning and capabilities for sharing maritime missions. A special JCG task force at the eleventh regional headquarters in Okinawa has responsibility for the Senkaku/Diaoyu area, and a U.S. liaison team could be assigned there as well as onboard JCG vessels. Data links and other communications upgrades could be added, along with real-time exercises between the JCG and MSDF, which could include consultations with relevant U.S. forces.

Risk-Reduction Measures for the East China Sea

Crisis management protocols are needed for Chinese and Japanese maritime and aerial forces in the East China Sea. The United States can encourage a bilateral agreement between Japan and China along the lines of the U.S.-China Military Maritime Consultative Agreement. In May 2012, the first Japan-China High-Level Consultation on Maritime Affairs was held in Hangzhou, China, and in June, Tokyo and Beijing concluded an agreement to establish crisis communications, including a hotline. Japan and China can be encouraged to restart this initiative and push forward with consultations on a search-and-rescue agreement. A multilateral code of conduct in the East China Sea, modeled on the Association of Southeast Asian Nations (ASEAN) code of conduct in the South China Sea, could also be considered. This would require participation by South Korea, in addition to Japan and China, and could be pursued in trilateral China-South Korea-Japan talks or in a new forum with Chinese, Japanese, South Korean, and U.S. participation.

Military interactions between Japanese and Chinese forces can also be more predictable if regular bilateral military-to-military consultations are held. Recent tensions with China have increased worries in Tokyo about China's long-term intentions. To ease these heightened concerns, the United States could encourage Beijing to be more transparent about its maritime strategy and strategic goals.

Diplomatic Efforts to Manage (or Resolve) the Territorial Dispute

Preventing armed conflict between Japan and China over the Senkaku/Diaoyu Islands dispute ultimately depends on Beijing and Tokyo finding a mutually acceptable framework for managing their differences. An active diplomatic effort to embed the island dispute in a stronger and more constructive Japan-China relationship will be needed and could be encouraged by Washington.

Several options exist for managing the dispute. The first, and most preferable, is a bilateral diplomatic effort. Since 1978, both governments have sought to control their citizens from seeking access to the islands. The Japanese government's decision to preempt activist purchase of the islands does not preclude a return to the status quo ante.

Second, Washington could encourage Beijing and Tokyo to explore new collaborative formulas for managing their island dispute. Developing proposals for transforming the islands into a nature preserve or some other entity that would restrict human access could also offer a way to demilitarize the dispute. However, this approach seems unlikely to attract attention in either Beijing or Tokyo at the moment.

Third, if the dispute cannot be managed peacefully through bilateral negotiations, Japan and China could be encouraged to seek international adjudication. The International Court of Justice (ICJ) could be asked to open a hearing. Beijing, having challenged Japan's sovereignty claim in 1971, should initiate the ICJ adjudication process. Washington should not expect Tokyo to take the first step, but should encourage Tokyo to respond if Beijing were to submit the dispute for international mediation.

Finally, Japan and China could be encouraged to develop cooperation in the management of their East China Sea maritime boundary. The East China Sea is 360 nautical miles wide, falling short of the 400 nautical miles that would be required to enforce the UN Convention on the Law of the Sea (UNCLOS), which defined 200-mile exclusive economic zones. While Japan argues for the establishment of a median line halfway between the two coastlines, China argues for an exclusive economic zone based on its extended continental shelf. This contested maritime boundary exacerbates the unpredictability of interactions between Japanese and Chinese forces across the East China Sea. Japan and China should be urged to implement their 2008 joint development agreement for exploring hydrocarbon resources in the East China Sea to build trust and cooperation in maritime management.

MITIGATING OPTIONS

Should a military conflict erupt between China and Japan, the United States can react in several ways to contain and minimize the threat to its interests. The U.S. response would depend on the scale of the armed clash. Options for U.S. policymakers include:

- *Urge Tokyo to stand down.* Withholding U.S. military support could change Japan's strategic calculus in the context of a conflict. This option would create a severe backlash against the United States in Japan and fatally undermine the bilateral alliance. Appeasing Beijing would also embolden China to use force against other U.S. allies in the region.

- *Contain any inadvertent incident involving the use of force.* In the event of an incident between Japanese and Chinese forces, Washington could immediately use all means at its disposal to communicate to both Tokyo and Beijing its interest in preventing an armed clash from escalating. The U.S. military could offer search-and-rescue assistance for any vessel and crew involved in an armed clash. Communications with Beijing may prove difficult, but all means, including the hotline and crisis communication mechanisms outlined in the U.S.-China Military Maritime Consultative Agreement, could be used to encourage a stand-down of forces. Real-time communication between Japan's chief of joint staff and the commander of U.S. Forces–Japan will make local military coordination with Tokyo easier, but immediate attention should be given to communication between the U.S. president and the Japanese prime minister on how to control the situation.

- *Plan for southwestern island contingency in U.S.-Japan defense cooperation.* Washington and Tokyo could continue regular exercises and planning to deter, and, if necessary, defend Japan against an armed attack. Japan may ask the United States to assist should China unilaterally opt to take military action to occupy the disputed islands. The scale and timing of that assistance will depend on the scale of attack. If the conflict were to expand beyond the disputed islands to become an all-out military clash between Japan and China, the United States should be prepared for integrated defense operations ranging from maritime and air defenses to ballistic missile defense as requested by Japan.

- *Call for an emergency session of the UN Security Council.* This option would engage the UN in the effort to de-escalate the crisis, although China's seat on the Security Council could limit the effectiveness of UN action. Nonetheless, the UN could facilitate a ceasefire and a negotiated end to hostilities.

- *Impose economic sanctions on Beijing.* Washington could impose sanctions on financial transactions, the movement of goods and services, and travel between China and the United States. However, China can retaliate in kind by barring U.S. exports, curtailing or ending purchases of U.S. treasuries, and limiting investment flows.

- *Threaten China with a U.S. military response to any use of force against Japan.* Washington could adopt a strategy of escalating any use of force to gain control over the Senkaku/Diaoyu Islands into a U.S.-Japan coordinated response designed to repel Chinese forces and establish Japanese military control over the disputed islands. This could severely damage the United States' relations with China.

RECOMMENDATIONS

The United States should pursue three policy goals: promote de-escalation of the dispute, initiate crisis management consultations with Japan, and intensify efforts to create multilateral maritime risk reduction mechanisms in the Asia-Pacific region. More specifically:

- *The United States should consistently and clearly reiterate its treaty obligation to assist in Japan's defense if China uses force to resolve the dispute over the islands.* Until the risk of miscalculations subsides between Japan and China, the United States should continue to make clear its long-standing position that the Senkaku/Diaoyu Islands are covered by the U.S.-Japan security treaty.

- *The United States should continue to encourage China and Japan to seek peaceful resolution of the dispute and remind Beijing that the unilateral actions of other powers will not change U.S. recognition of Japan's administrative control over the islands.* Secretary Clinton's January 18, 2013, statement, reiterated by

Secretary John Kerry on April 15 in Tokyo, offered a valuable clarification of the U.S. position. Washington should condemn harshly the use of force to settle this dispute.

- *The United States should urge Japan and China to avoid any steps that might escalate tensions in and around the disputed islands.* Washington should encourage Tokyo to continue to avoid populating the islands or deploying military forces to defend its control so long as there are no efforts by Beijing to seize control of the islands. The United States should encourage China to restart High-Level Consultations on Maritime Affairs with Japan and to implement their agreement to establish crisis management communications.

- *The United States should continue to advocate for transparency between maritime forces in the East China Sea and the development of mechanisms for confidence building.* As China's maritime power grows, greater comfort with the procedures and prohibitions on interactions with military and nonmilitary vessels, including aircraft, across this increasingly crowded sea will be required. Opportunities for Chinese participation must be expanded in existing regional maritime cooperation, such as the annual Rim of the Pacific exercises, regular regional fisheries exercises, and coast guard exercises dedicated to search-and-rescue operations and humanitarian assistance. The United States should also encourage the countries of Northeast Asia to develop Incidents at Sea agreements.

- *Should China initiate the use of force against Japan, the United States should be fully prepared to provide military assistance to Japan.* The United States should maintain the requisite capability and readiness to fulfill its commitment to assist in defending Japan.

- *The United States and Japan should develop clear alliance crisis management procedures for an incident or armed clash in and around the disputed islands.* Washington and Tokyo should design plans to manage a military clash between Japanese and Chinese militaries, including how to control escalation and communicate effectively with Beijing. Past U.S. and Japanese incidents with Chinese forces should be closely examined as the basis of an alliance response. Containing escalation should be the highest priority for alliance crisis management.

- *The United States and Japan should continue to improve defense consultations and exercises designed to enhance Japan's southwestern defenses.* The island dispute exacerbates an increasing trend of interaction between Chinese and Japanese forces in Japan's southwest. As Chinese naval strength grows, these interactions are likely to increase, raising concern that Chinese military presence in and around Japan could impinge on the United States' ability to assist in Japan's defense. Washington and Tokyo should improve ISR and amphibious landing cooperation and strengthen Japan's air defenses.

- *The United States should strongly encourage China to expand consultations with its maritime neighbors on its evolving strategy.* China's rise is creating deep uncertainty about its longer-term intentions regarding the use of its military power. Washington should continue regular regional security consultations in the ASEAN Regional Forum and encourage annual meetings of regional defense ministers. Open sea lanes, including antipiracy operations, are the lifelines of Asia's growing economy, and the United States should continue to advocate freedom of navigation.

- *Finally, the United States should ratify the UN Convention on the Law of the Sea in order to become a more forceful actor in global deliberations over maritime rights and sovereignty dispute resolution.* In both the East and South China Seas, China's neighbors are seeking the adjudication of maritime disputes in UNCLOS. The United States cannot shape the maritime debate in the Asia Pacific or defend its own maritime interests if it is not a full participant in international maritime deliberations.

The Center for Preventive Action (CPA) seeks to help prevent, defuse, or resolve deadly conflicts around the world and to expand the body of knowledge on conflict prevention. The CPA Contingency Roundtable and Memoranda series seek to organize focused discussions on plausible short- to medium-term contingencies that could seriously threaten U.S. interests. Contingency meeting topics range from specific states or regions of concern to more thematic issues and draw on the expertise of government and nongovernment experts.

The Council on Foreign Relations acknowledges the Rockefeller Brothers Fund for its generous support of the Contingency Planning Roundtables and Memoranda.

The Council on Foreign Relations (CFR) is an independent, nonpartisan membership organization, think tank, and publisher dedicated to being a resource for its members, government officials, business executives, journalists, educators and students, civic and religious leaders, and other interested citizens in order to help them better understand the world and the foreign policy choices facing the United States and other countries.

The Council on Foreign Relations takes no institutional positions on policy issues and has no affiliation with the U.S. government. All statements of fact and expressions of opinion contained in its publications are the sole responsibility of the author or authors.

For further information about CFR or this paper, please write to the Council on Foreign Relations, 58 East 68th Street, New York, NY 10065, or call Communications at 212.434.9888. Visit CFR's website, www.cfr.org.